Psychology

By Dr. Edward Schellhammer
Founder and President of MARBELLA UNIVERSITY

8. Edition 2012, revised
© Copyright 2012. Dr. Edward Schellhammer.
All Rights Reserved.

ISBN-13: 978-1478370666
ISBN-10: 1478370661

www.MarbellaUniversity.com
www.PioneeringEducation.com

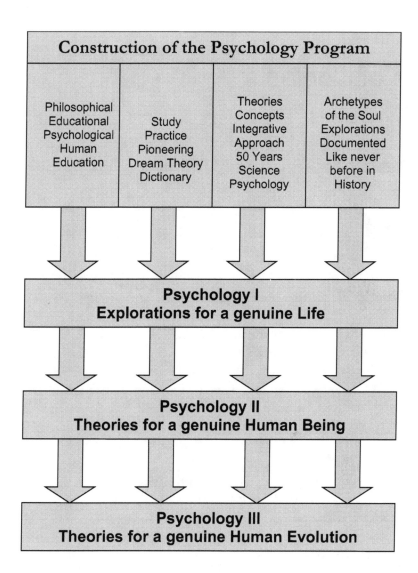

Construction of the Psychology Program

| Philosophical Educational Psychological Human Education | Study Practice Pioneering Dream Theory Dictionary | Theories Concepts Integrative Approach 50 Years Science Psychology | Archetypes of the Soul Explorations Documented Like never before in History |

Psychology I
Explorations for a genuine Life

Psychology II
Theories for a genuine Human Being

Psychology III
Theories for a genuine Human Evolution

Table of Contents

List of Diagrams

In Somnis Veritas for Psychology I

Dreams tell the truth. Dreams stand above theories, ideologies and dogmas. During the last 33 years I have had over 12,000 dreams about the state of humanity and the planet. I had an estimated 3,000 dreams about the evolution of humans and all processes of the Archetypes of the Soul.

Examples:

A voice: "Also for the rich people tomorrow, no risks will be covered."

An unknown town in Northern Europe. Everywhere men show their penis, some are partly and some completely naked, partly covered with cloth or plastic. Many have blown their penis up with air, technically enlarged, even some little boys. They show each other the 'marvelous' thing they have. Many women are totally excited over these men with big and large penises. Everything seems like carnival. I observe from a distance, find this disgusting, distasteful, an expression of the sick society.

One can ignite the entire world with one bomb.

Tornados. Floods. Waves up to 30 and even 100 meters. Massive. It destroys everything into 1000 pieces. I am somewhere, entirely in the light.

Young people don't want to learn, least of all about self-knowledge and reflection. Only by force.

An assembly. I tell the people: Not taking serious the values and realities of the psychical life is deadly for the entire collective.

In Zurich. Millions of very small maggots everywhere. They devour people's bodies.

Earthquakes. Floods. Masses of people falling into abysm. Agitations everywhere.

A big town such as Berlin: Neurotic people, psychopaths, amusement parks...
...Masses of monkeys dancing everywhere, people with drive disturbances, politicians, people from the show business, and also people from the culture. All decadent!

A huge ship like Titanic, but even bigger. 35,000 people are on it. It's sailing. It's night. Then, an incident, and the ship slowly sinks.

I am standing on a bridge. There is a river underneath, flowing from a lake. It is raining incessantly. The water level is rising. I see that there is an enormous catastrophe approaching.

I receive a sword, a scepter, a globe and a cross; these symbols I compose into a circle-cross-Mandala.

I receive a goblet and I am summoned to search the mysteries of life in it.

A sun-like female figure draws me towards it, embraces me and I can feel its energy flowing through me like a strong current. Then I'm unified with this light, I am one with this sun. "This is the unio mystica", it is said.

I am in the Garden of Eden. It is indescribably beautiful. The paradise is mine. It is within me.

I am on my way to the universe; I must cross a bridge and I have to promise to go back to the people, then I meet God (a burning well); I can see pyramids of light, golden worlds and a huge golden circle-cross-Mandala shimmering on the eternal horizon. 'Death', who is the only witness of my journey to God, says: "Fulfilled is the word."

The truth and the Archetypes of the Soul are the primordial foundation and aim of science, human life, and society. 'Psychology doesn't have either of them! The entire social sciences do not have them. That's the scandalous drama of science.

The absence of the truth and of the Archetypes of the Soul produces enormous destructive energy and developments in sciences and societies.

It shows clearly that sciences do not take care of the archetypal, psychical and spiritual evolution of mankind nor do they have any respect for the creation.

Such science is a sham. Such sciences dehumanize mind and soul, and eliminate the dignity of humans.

Such sciences are infected with the most toxic virus ever existed: the dynamic code for regicide and deicide. In the end, it will irreversibly and unstoppably lead to the total collapse.

It can happen within decades if drastic measures around the globe are not taken soon.

Dr. Edward Schellhammer

Introduction

Psychological Explorations and the Foundation of Personality

Personality education means 'to form oneself'. This has got a lot to do with the psychical life. One can acquire knowledge from the sciences of psychology, philosophy and pedagogy (education), without acquiring any real self-education.

Therefore: Studying Psychology is a systematic experience and elaboration of all own psychical forces. This challenge is more than just a taking in thoughts of knowledge about the human being. Psychology also means: to develop, to grow, and to change.

Many may think: "Why should I educate myself by studying Psychology? I know myself well and I am sufficiently educated." That is a difficult situation: What one doesn't know and doesn't see for himself, doesn't exist as a reality. Others may experience their inner life as something dark, a depth without boundaries. One better doesn't look there. Yet this is wrong.

All psychical forces are identifiable and in that sense limitable. The psychical life of the human being is very rich. There one can discover a lot, much more than most people may consider as possible. By studying Psychology these discoveries add a deepened value and sense to life.

We are all thoroughly educated, trained and formed from the early childhood. 'Enough now' many may think, 'it is time to live'. "I want to study Psychology and not to be challenged personally for self-knowledge and personal development". Much of what people learn during the first 20 years may be useful for the whole life. But a lot is childlike and not useful for life. We all have to learn new things, again and again depending on the stage of life and the challenges that life presents. A lot about ourselves we do not learn neither at home nor in school.

The psychical life in general remains an undiscovered reality. That this reality exists, everyone can feel every day. It often acts vaguely, disturbing, annoying and uncontrollable. The effects of the psychical life are recognizable and often bitter to feel.

In primary school they teach a lot about mathematics, language, geography, history and other subjects. Why shouldn't children also learn about the 'geography of the psychical life'? Why shouldn't young people learn, how to understand and to take their own psychical forces seriously.

Why shouldn't adolescents before leaving school, learn how one can and should care for the psychical life of others? The same question goes for adults: Why shouldn't students and in general all adults learn about a complete self-knowledge, human knowledge and the process of Individuation?

Knowing all your own psychical forces and forming them so that they prove useful in life, instead of causing damage is well worth it. Life is easier if one knows the psychical inner world, and can guide these psychical forces, like a captain his ship. One can only steer, what one knows and what one has integrated into the ego-guidance. Every one is what life has 'made' of him.

Everyone carries with him his whole lived life. If this inner life isn't integrated in the consciousness, isn't elaborated, cleared and formed anew, then it acts like inner chains. This in turn hinders the process of becoming conscious about one's own life potentials. Potentials lie unused and cannot grow. The human being remains a prisoner of his upbringing and education, without recognizing the great value of a true inner freedom. In that sense studying Psychology can make free.

Extensive self-knowledge is the start to all opportunities in life. If we comprehend all the psychical 'sub-systems' within us, then we can systematically build up a holistic personality education.

If we know all the methods of knowledge and education, then we have the tools to form our psychical life. If we know how the psychical forces grow and how they can be changed, then the path of this educational process is clearly definable. The journey of discovery can start: the plan, the instruments and the aims are determined.

The discovery of the self-identity, the growth of the personality, the thorough knowledge about the human being and the systematic self-discovery are decisive for wellbeing and professional success. Those people that do not suppress their inner life and devote themselves to the psychical life can develop their prospects. Personality education and life training are more important then ever, because the human being is to a large extent a psychical being.

It is important to find distance to the daily life, to reduce stress and to concentrate new forces. Inner freedom is found by those that put their emotions, thoughts and life experiences into order. A cooperative love relationship with a satisfied sexuality is a fortune that can be elaborated. Knowledge of human beings starts with self-analysis. It is smart to solve conflicts with oneself and with life. The relationships at the workplace, in the personal love relationship and the social life include communication skills and the whole personality in its development. Social competences and work techniques are therefore essential for personal and professional success.

Herewith we see clearly: Psychology is of highest importance in human's life. In addition to that, Personality development demands several other operations:

Important parts of Psychology, ignored by most scientific concepts, are: The integration of the shadows and the (psychical) opposite gender, the entire elaboration of the unconscious (and the biography), the development of all potentials and the archetypical transformations until the realization of the supreme 'Mandala' (a symbol that expresses the aim of human evolution). These transformations guide the human being to the basic questions of existence which are answered with the archetypical experiences during the process of a holistic development, called 'Individuation'.

Individuation transforms the inner oppositions to a constructive interaction of all psychical forces. This is a psychical-spiritual process that is founded and rooted in the spiritual intelligence, called: the Inner Spirit. Individuation is realization of life with Spirit. The freedom of thinking and being free from neurosis allows for an authentic and creative self-realization.

Therefore Individuation is not the same as Individualization. The term 'Individualization' refers to a philosophical system, which considers the person as a purpose of all laws, of all moral and political networks. The term 'Individuation' is predominantly used in analytical psychology. But: Individuation is not a psychotherapeutic technique, and is not suitable for psychiatric illnesses. Individuation is a concept of personal development and of human education in general.

This book forms the foundation to understand the psychological factors of humans' life. This is the first phase of studying Psychology. The chapters are all constructed in the same way: Every subject consists of three parts, each with a text complemented with short statements and keywords for reflection and discussion, and with a diagram for an overview. This basic knowledge is enhanced with learning material from scientific literature and from collected knowledge. Every unit ends with exercises. Then a small multiple choice test follows.

The Beginning of Psychology

Each human being is what life has made of him, and what he makes of himself from his possibilities. So the first question is: What did you become until today? And above all, from another point of view: What didn't you become?

Do you know 'Who' ('What') you are? Do you know your inner potentials? Do you understand your thinking, your feelings, your needs, your unconscious life, your dreams, and your force of love?

Don't ever say that this is unimportant. Don't refuse it by leaving 'wisdom' to others. If you receive the 'gold' and the 'jewels' of the psychical-spiritual life in your hands, then take it up with seriousness and dignity. Take good care of it.

You want to understand life; certainly your own life. That is a difficult concern. There are countless religions, philosophies and psychological concepts, which claim to offer the 'true path'. Critical vigilance and profound knowledge are necessary.

Look into your mirror: for a long time, systematically and with precise empathy. Only the one, who looks into his own 'depths', can find love, the Spirit, and humility, which are necessary in order to understand oneself, others and the meaning of existence. Being self-critical is not easy.

It will be exciting for the one who begins to discover himself thoroughly and extensively. Nothing can create as much inner peace as truthfulness through personality education and the Individuation process.

Our world needs many people, who educate themselves, who jointly take responsibility for the basic values of the psychical-spiritual life, and those who realize that which gives our future a chance: becoming a vivid representation of the circle-cross-archetype.

Your self-education is the most important and valuable 'work' of your human life. With this first step in the Individuation process you will meet the necessary preparations. You will elaborate the basic foundations for life with plans, aims, steps, methods, elementary knowledge and the first applications.

Studying Psychology is challenging in many ways. First of all, the student is permanently challenged by himself to understand psychological functions.

Secondly, the more a student understands psychological realities, the more he becomes aware of the importance of psychology in human's life.

In this program we explore humans' ways of living that is far away from a genuine living and development.

Humanity has already lost the truth and the essential genuine human values, in the same way as the science of Psychology.

The Essence

To understand Psychology one needs to identify the psychological realities in the everyday life of humans. To see the importance of psychology one needs to be aware of the result of people's ways of acting, thinking, and living.

There are two psychological factors of immense impact:

1) The efficiency of the operating psychical functions of people; and

2) The meaning of the psychical functions related to a general meaning of life between two poles: Regression and Progression.

Living on this earth is a precious gift. But if people do not shape all their mental and spiritual functions for an efficient progression, then they destroy themselves and the entire psychical-spiritual evolution of humanity.

If we explore the psychical and real world, we can already see a fatal dehumanization, a complete inefficiency of humans' living, and an upcoming global disaster.

The science of Psychology (also of Education and Philosophy) is in a lamentable state: A huge majority of Psychology professors at universities, including those with super-best reputation, know themselves on a level of maximum 10-20%; some individuals might know themselves up to 35%.

If the goal of the psychical-spiritual development as the reached, totality and completeness can be marked with the level of 100%, then these professors and experts, including Freudians and Jungians, have reached in the best case a level of 20%, some unknown individuals maybe up to 45%.

Many of these experts are very narcissistic and neurotic; some psychopaths are everywhere. It is really necessary that those who study psychology never lose sight of this scandalous situation.

Furthermore everybody must know: The goal is reachable! If people don't want the path towards this goal, then this converts into a collective program of regression until the elimination of the human evolution.

Herewith we make clear how important Psychology is for each human and for humanity.

All the instruments to explore Psychology in real life are now in your hands.

Good luck!

1. Human Images

The more a person takes the psychical life seriously, the more genuine and truthful his life will become in all areas.

Essential Theses

❑ Every human being has psychical forces. These can be put together into the following sub-systems:

- Intelligence (cognitive)
- Unconscious
- Ego/Consciousness
- Feelings
- Love
- Psycho-Dynamism
- Needs
- Spiritual Intelligence
- Actions

❑ Every psychical sub-system contains different singular psychical forces and forms of expression.

❑ All psychical forces and sub-systems act together and influence each other, mostly without people recognizing it consciously.

❑ Psychical forces and sub-systems together form a systematic wholeness, we define this as: 'the psychical organism'.

❑ The holistic image of human beings is based on that psychical organism ('system'), which can be developed with different scientific methods.

❑ Every system of ideas (psychological, pedagogical, spiritual, philosophical, and religious) about man is only worth as much as the wholeness of the psychical-spiritual existence of human beings that is effectively realized in the external life.

1.1. The Human and his Psychical Life

The sciences of Psychology, Pedagogy, Andragogy (= theory of adult education) and Philosophy deal with the psychical life. Even in ancient times, in all early advanced civilizations, people thought and philosophized about the mysterious psychical inner world.

What exactly is this 'inner world' about?
What do we mean, when we speak about the 'psychical life'?

We think, perhaps, about 'intelligence' and envisage something to do with thought processes. Everybody thinks and gives labels to these thoughts with words. We all have a rich experience of feelings. Joy, happiness, lust and peace are classical positive feelings.

Everybody also has aggressive feelings, goes through hopelessness and loneliness. Most of us experience love as a feeling. But the force of love is more than a feeling.

We all need love for a constructive life. Love can reconcile and stimulate us to great performances beyond the needs of lust. Most of the needs are 'psychological'.

We all have a need to be accepted, for self-realization, for a deeper sense of life, for peace, for security. If we looking around in our consumer society, we get the impression that many needs are artificially suggested.

Every one of us has a personal characteristic of psycho-dynamism, a psycho-energetic state of relaxation and tension, of calm and restlessness, of vitality and laziness.

Subsequently we all have an 'unconscious' reality in our inner life. Everything that we have experienced since our earliest days is stored as pictures in our 'unconscious' memory.

These are general experiences, norms, threats, punishments, attitudes and many images about the human being and life.

The 'conscience' is a part of our unconscious inner world. Many of this we can remember. The main part however can only be remembered with specific methods.

Our consciousness is part of our psychical life. We have a consciousness about others, about the earth and perhaps about the divine. The 'ego' can decide, what shall come into our 'screen', our consciousness: memories, thoughts, feelings, perceptions and many more. The ego can also reject to see, to hear, to feel and to act. The ego can want, wish, manage and decide.

Everybody has dreams every night, but many people just cannot remember their dreams. The inner visual perception, the day-dreaming and the fantasizing are also a kind of dream. Since the early days of yore the philosophers and the wise teach us, that a spiritual force is speaking in dreams to the ego - warning, advising and guiding man through life. We call this force 'the inner Spirit' in the human being.

→ This short overview tells us that psychological factors are everywhere in humans' life.

Reflections and Discussion

■ No doubt, everybody occasionally uses terms like 'psychical', 'Psychology', 'psychological', 'inner life' and other similar words. Many psychological words are common in our daily language: dreams, unconscious, meditation, perception, thinking ...

Which words do people use every now and then in their daily communication (with their partner, friends, children, acquaintances, at work, etc.)?

■ Most people react critically to all psychical subjects, as soon as somebody starts to talk about this subject, often with:

▪ Indifference	▪ Mockery	▪ Scoff
▪ Rejection	▪ Disregard	▪ Cynicism
▪ Oppression	▪ Escape	▪ Jokes
▪ Denial	▪ Depreciation	▪ Defense

How do we have to interpret such reactions from people in general?

■ We all know a diversity of words, which concern the psychical life; here are some examples:

▪ Thinking	▪ Dreams	▪ Will
▪ Inner Needs	▪ Unconscious	▪ Wishes
▪ Life Force	▪ Consciousness	▪ Integration
▪ Ego	▪ Feelings	▪ Language
▪ Attitudes	▪ Love	▪ Daydreams, Fantasies
▪ Rejection	▪ Psychical Energy	▪ Memory
▪ Perception	▪ Conscience	▪ Action/Behavior

What is the picture people in general have about such words?

■ Some facts about the psychical life are:

- Many things in our life are 'psychical'.
- Everybody has a psychical life.
- We all have many individual psychical forces.
- Everything that we do has got to do with our psychical life.
- We can't define the human being without psychical life.

■ The importance of the psychical life:

1. How do people in general manage these psychical forces?
2. What is a human that does not use his thinking capacities?
3. What is a human that does not care for his feelings?
4. What is a human that does ignore the capacity of love?
5. What are the consequences if a human does not control his behavior?
6. What happens if the perception of a human is very selected and superficial?

Diagram 1.1: Psychical Forces of Humans

What is Psychology? What does 'Psyche' mean?

We take some (German) dictionaries, look up the keywords and put the information together:

Psyche: Soul, the life of the soul; the innermost nature, the mind, the individual characteristic.

From Hellenic: expiration, breath, soul as the subject of conscious experiences.

Psychology: Science or teaching about experience and behavior and about the significant inner forces that from expression.

Philosophical Psychology asks about spirituality, substance, body, freedom, immortality (metaphysics).

Empirical Psychology investigates: psychical manifestations, motivation, expression, relationships.

Psychology: The science which investigates the regularity of the psychical processes and of the psychical quality (features) in their interdependency from the environment (milieu, social background).

Psychology: Knowledge about inner (mental) life, science about (mental) inner life; exists as a scientific term since the beginning of the 18th century (Humanism). The thinking about psychical/psychological questions exists since early history.

Today we have more then 18,000 words which express psychical facts; in one small dictionary we can find more than 5,000 defined terms.

Psyche: Life, soul, mind. Psychology: is the science which investigates the conscious processes and states, also the causes and effects.

Basic principles of the psyche (mind) are:

1) Proceedings (not something steady)
2) Vivid appearances, links to a unit (individual), dependency between one another (holistic constitution), individual appearances (accommodation, heredity)
3) Subjectivity: only the person can experience in himself the inner state and processes

4) Connections: psychical (mental) processes are linked with physical processes (e.g. the brain)

In addition there are numerous different psychologies; here a selection:

▪ Developmental Psychology	▪ Depth Psychology
▪ Industrial Psychology	▪ Psychotherapy
▪ Learning Psychology	▪ Humanistic Psychology
▪ Sports Psychology	▪ Advertising Psychology
▪ Behavioral psychology	▪ Psychology
▪ Philosophical Psychology	▪ Ethno Psychology
▪ Family Psychology	▪ Social Psychology
▪ Environmental Psychology	▪ Cultural Psychology
▪ Analytical Psychology	▪ Political
▪ Clinical Psychology	▪ Animal Psychology

Psychological Questions in the Context of Personality

What?

What are feelings?
What does 'lust' mean?
What is the 'unconscious'?
What happens between two loving/hostile people?
What is intelligence?
What is thinking?
What occurs inside?
What does "self-realization" mean?
What are psychical needs?

How?

How does certain behavior come about?
How is the will formed?
How does the conscience evolve?
How does knowledge affect self-guidance?
How does self-identity develop?
How does perception work?
How can one improve one's capacity of performance?
How can we activate "good feelings"?
How can one change oneself?

Why?

Why do differences in the intellectual performance exist?
Why does one person become depressed because of X, while others react differently?
Why do people not care for their Psyche?
Why does one strive for money; another one strive for inner experiences about God?
Why does a person react with stress-symptoms, while another reacts with calmness?
Why do many people suppress their sexual lust-impulses?
Why do some people become aggressive, violent or belligerent?
Why are people unhappy?
Why do people project?
Why does the biography have a lasting effect on the present and future?
Why do many people suppress their feelings?
Why does one chose one person and not another as the life partner?
Why does the human being play?
Why should one think about oneself?
Why is meditation meaningful?
Why are dreams important?
Why should human beings continue to develop themselves?

What for? Where?

What are dreams good for?
What is the unconscious there for?
Where does psychical growth and development lead to?
What do "roles" serve for?
What is imagination useful for?
What do religious feelings provide?
What should we practice intuition for?
Where does indifference towards the psychical life lead to?

Notes and Perspectives

What purpose does psychology serve in daily life?

Write down the central keywords from this sub-chapter:

What is the human being without his psychical life?

Explain: Knowledge about the psychical life is important because…:

What do people learn about Psychology in their parent's home, at school and in the church?

What importance does psychological knowledge have in the communication between life partners and in social interactions in general?

How do politics and the economy benefit from the psychological knowledge?

What does advertising convey to us about the psychical life?

Formulate some questions about Psychology that are important to you:

1.2. Manifoldness of Human Images

Most people live predominantly without a reflective consciousness about their human image. They don't ask about the psychical reality. As a substitute they have prejudices, ideologies and dogmatic doctrines.

Everyone has his own philosophy, his own 'theory' about human beings, about life and God. A transcendental reality exists for some people; not for others.

The teachings about human beings are always developed from the psychical-spiritual state of these teachers. In the everyday life people often give others animal names. Those selling products see other people as buyers.

Those looking after governmental business see human beings as a mass that has to be guided with power instruments. Those who possess nothing perceive others as the proprietors. Those who go to church, see those who don't as godless people. He, who studies philosophy in his room, develops his ideas about human beings according to some sort of tradition and his way of thinking. The doctor sees the patient and the injured. The psychotherapist analyses psychical disorders.

Every psychologist sees those around according to his studied theories. One is analyzing the behavior; others are looking for the depth of the soul. Priests see everything in the light of dogmas. A teacher experiences his students as learners. Whites differentiate from blacks. The fundamentalist is limited in his perception by 'holy' texts.

Everywhere people see others as alien, that is to say, as those who don't fit in with their own 'theories' and 'right' ideas. Everything starts with psychology and everything is seen in some psychological way.

There are many people all around the Earth, and have always been, who want to explore and get to the bottom of human nature and existence. We have a need to understand ourselves and our life. We search for sense and values. We live between procreation and death.

The question of a valuable image of human beings is a very serious matter for our forms of living and for our (self-) education.

People have their own images about human beings depending on their position, their mental state and their life history. Most people don't want to change or widen their images about humans. They don't see, that their images seize less than one percent of the human reality. Then there are those that expect others should coincide with their images. If they don't do so, they are seen as hostile.

Many people teach numerous images about human beings and a lot of ideas of how life has to be lived. That provokes tensions between humans. This causes aggressions and violence. Wars are also a result of this.

If people would widen their image of human beings, then new hopeful ways would be opened. The paths start with learning about the psychological dimensions and this automatically includes a certain self-knowledge.

Reflections and Discussion

■ We all have images about human beings in our mind, partly as simple patterns of images, partly as prejudices, partly as well-founded theory. The whole history of philosophy and education is also a history of changing images of human beings. Let's touch on some sketches:

- A human is from his nature good and bad
- A human is the wolf of the man
- A human is God's image
- A human is the species which has a will
- A human is the undiscovered animal
- A human is the sick animal
- A human is the first to be freed from nature
- A human is a defective creature
- A human is a social creature
- A human is the animal which can create wars
- A human is a biological creature
- A human is what education and environment has made him
- A human is the creature that can think
- A human is the highest creation of God
- A human is lazy, incalculable, lying, and egoistic
- A human is a spiritual creature
- A human is a driven creature
- A human is a creature that can create culture
- A human is the 'homo faber', talented for technique
- A human is the 'homo sapiens', endowed with reason

- A human is the 'homo ludens', a 'player'
- A human is able to think
- A human is able to love
- A human is needy and capable of being educated
- A human is a creature which can sin
- A human is pure race, or is impure race
- A human is a learning organism

■ If we look to psychology, we find the 'healthy', the 'neurotic', the 'psychopathic', the 'narcissistic' human.

In earlier times they classified humans in typologies, for example:

Melancholic, choleric, sanguine, phlegmatic; or in another typology: religious, economical, aesthetical, social, theoretical and the power-man; or in a further typology: the Dionysian and Apollo-like man; or the 'pyknic'-type, the leptosome and the athletic man.

Which terms do people use sometimes and why do they use these words?

Images about human beings are psychological, philosophical, theological, pedagogical, esoteric, biological, economical, and sociological.

Sometimes people also use animal names such as 'monkey', 'chicken', 'snake', 'pig', 'dog', and many more.

Make a list with more examples and note the meaning people give to such words.

Diagram 1.2: Aspects of Viewing Humans

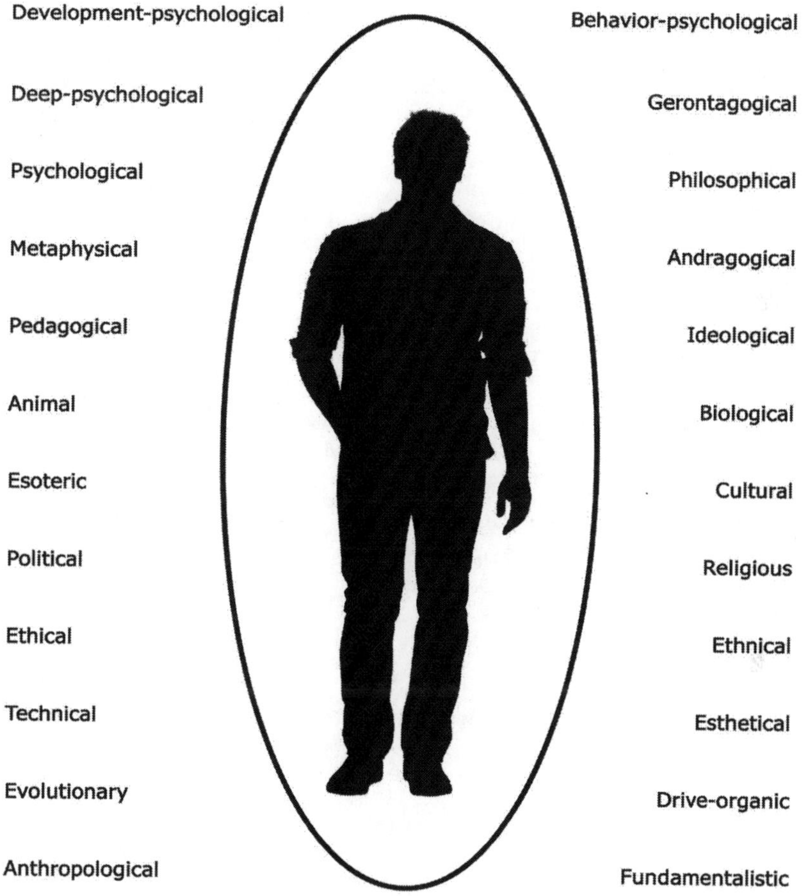

Development-psychological	Behavior-psychological
Deep-psychological	Gerontagogical
Psychological	Philosophical
Metaphysical	Andragogical
Pedagogical	Ideological
Animal	Biological
Esoteric	Cultural
Political	Religious
Ethical	Ethnical
Technical	Esthetical
Evolutionary	Drive-organic
Anthropological	Fundamentalistic

The Classical Human Image in our Époque

Many people claim: 'I don't have problems'. A reality filled with problems shall not be. What else isn't 'allowed' in the social network of people? The farther away one is in the desired conceivability of others, the more one is inclined to present oneself, the way others demand. This happens with clothes, goods, cars, career, and money and with the adaptation of one's own attitudes. The reality in one's consciousness is defined by social pressure. That is how 'life lies' are created.

Most people don't want to see how their ego masters life. The tendency to harmonize external realities ("all that cannot be so important and so bad") may relax the situation for a moment. But it is not possible to build up enduring foundation of life like that. This is because the separated (suppressed) reality is present and working in full gear: from inside and from outside, from oneself and from others. Like a flood, the unperceived reality inundates each single person as well as the collective; with suffering, social conflicts, criminality, destruction of environment, and wars.

Life lies in the core are self-denial, suppression of one's own and of other's psychical life. The person doesn't want to know about his own real psychical being, ignores his inner being and rejects the real problems. Life lies are always an escape from one-self. Life lies force a person to self-alienation and to manifold suffering. This is because the separation of the inner psychical life creates tension and therefore also neurotic conflicts. Life lies produce a lot of unnecessary self-tortures.

The life lie is a self-deception: the person is cheating his inner being and his life; he is permanently pressed from his need to be loved, acknowledged and admired. He can't live from his inner source of life, but only from the value others and the social community give him. With life lies the cheated person is rarely only a victim. He lives himself in the life lie. He plays together with others using camouflaging projections. He is adapted in the values and attitudes of his environment. Denying one's self favors the social norms (zeitgeist). He, who is victim of life lies, mostly is also too trusting.

The person in the life lie is primarily his own perpetrator. Given he accepts his life in lies. But this being is caused by the biography, starting from the early childhood, and promoted thoroughly during school years. The biggest epidemic in the pluralistic-democratic society is the life lie. Life lies corrode and destroy all truthful psychical-spiritual (evolutionary) human being.

The media play a very crucial role in the development of life lies, especially with adverts, but also with a large spectrum of films. They impart patterns of values which have, through permanent repetition, a high suggestive effect. The purpose of such adverts and trivial films is not to serve, but to manipulate: "Buy! Follow us!" In the core such patterns of values push the naïve person to escape from himself, and with that they promote going along with this collective manipulation: "Do, what we present you; that is the way you become happy, you find harmony, you get money and success." Such transferred patterns of values finally only serve the vendors that merely want all this for them. For that aim they need the people, and for that they manipulate them to find satisfaction with compensations (artificial needs).

The life lie is a way of repressing (ignoring, denying) the psychical-spiritual life. This always leads to manipulations of the collective: A person shall fulfill the given patterns. The churches demand it, the economists want it, the educational institutions want it, politics and the cultural society produce it, and the zeitgeist with all technical progresses stimulates it.

Truthful Life instead of Life Lies

Do people really want to know the 'truth'? That is first a question of Psychology and of self-knowledge. A person wants to know exactly as much about the truth as he wants to know about himself, and as prepared as he is (with psychological knowledge) to thoroughly practice self-knowledge. Let's look at it from another angle and develop some thoughts: Nobody wants psychological knowledge and self-knowledge, so nobody wants to know the truth anymore. Where does this lead in 50 or 100 years? By then most of us in our middle age today will not be alive anymore. Why should we care? What about our children? This should concern us!

Basically the problem about the truth starts in every daily life, in the relationship with oneself and with the partner. Tell your partner or your girlfriend or boyfriend: "I don't want to know the truth of your being!" Try and see how this works! Or maybe it's better to say nothing.

Nobody wants to tell others that he doesn't want to know the truth about himself and about others. That way we make the problem of the truth inexistent. And that's why Psychology produces fear to people. Psychology unveils the truth about human's inner life.

Where does it lead, if in a love relationship the partners already ignore the problem of rejecting the truth? Where does it lead to in society? It leads to a deeper entanglement in the life lie until nobody can even see that this life lies really exists. At that point a dialogue about life lies no longer exists. No dialogue about the truthful human being is the beginning of the destruction of mankind. In the end – in heaven – each soul will put the blame on others: "You also didn't talk about life lies." "If, at least, you would have started to talk about life lies." All souls will quarrel endlessly. Then all souls will have to start their psychical-spiritual evolution from zero as anthropoid apes, incarnating on another planet in the universe.

The life lies from every individual and from many products found in the media are simply a bluff. They bluff with their 'truth'. People delude others with a false reality, but declare this reality to be the 'truth'. Indeed, the one who is cheated is in a certain way at fault himself. The truth is often merely a pretended collective pattern. Furthermore, the truth is relative to a person. The truth is also conditioned by history. Given that, everything in our consciousness that we understand as the truth is in the consciousness because we have allowed it to be there. On top of that this reality is interpreted individually by each person.

The search for the truth has a psychological, philosophical and religious impact: The truth has got a lot to do with self-knowledge. A person first acknowledges his real face. If a person knows himself completely, he first recognizes his own truth. And he recognizes the truth of other people, because self-knowledge is the foundation of human knowledge. At the goal of the self-knowledge process there is the acknowledgement of God. Now, we have to see that self-knowledge is a process of growing. As a consequence we can say: Acknowledgement of God is finally the result of this growing process. In other words: Psychology leads to a transcendental dimension.

In the widest sense this means: The practiced psychology leads to the self-knowledge process and through the process of growth, ultimately to God; or the other way round: Without practicing psychology as a tool for self-knowledge, acknowledgement of God isn't possible. 'Practicing psychology' means: self-knowledge, personality education and Individuation. The alternative to life lies is the 'truth of life'.

Is this understanding of the truth correct? Do you want to know about it? Then, you must start this process of self-knowledge and you must explore your own inner world. That's the only way to prove it.

Notes and Perspectives

What purpose do human images serve in daily life?

Write down the central keywords from this sub-chapter:

What is the human being seen from psychological aspects?

Explain: Knowledge about human images is important because…:

What do people learn about human images in their parent's home, at school and in the church?

What importance do human images have in the communication between life partners and in social interactions in general?

How do politics and the economy benefit from human images?

What does advertising convey to us about human images?

Formulate some important questions about human images:

1.3. The Psychical Organism

Psychology offers us more than 50 theories about personality. This makes it difficult to find the 'right' image of human beings. On the other hand that is the chance:

If we confine within limits all theories, by understanding these as aspects of viewing and putting them together to a new wholeness, then we come closer to an image of human beings that is most likely to capture the entire reality of the psychical world.

The result of external experiences can be discussed. If many people give a detailed report, saying that they have systematically made their inner experiences, then we can also constructively discuss this inner world.

If we assume that there are different psychical realities, then the methods for inner experiences are also different. If we reach a minimal agreement and if we use well founded methods, then the ways are open for a holistic image of humans (mankind).

From that point of view and proceeding we can construct and define the 'psychical organism'. A first large model can be built.

We can then demand: Each image of man which doesn't contain all the identified components is a reduced model and has to be widened.

In the future Psychology and Education will discover many more aspects or describe the inner reality with new accents. Consequently we understand our model as innovative and dynamic: the model has to be constantly enlarged, to be constructed with new accents and to be defined with added terms in a wider light.

If we enlarge the knowledge of human beings, then the model of the psychical organism has to be widened too. Our model is an overview of the essential subsystems and its parts. When we speak about a human image, then all the elements from that system are an integrated constituent.

Each image of human beings, which excludes singular elements, must be rejected. Nobody constructs a car without wheels. No medicine teaches about the body without teaching about circulation. Cars are constantly developed further. Medicine is continuing with scientific research.

In the past 40 years Psychology and Education have not been significantly further developed.

Similarly the sciences of human beings have still got many questions to answer and many further methods to develop. This openness is a precondition, to talk about images of man constructively and to create our lives in that orientation.

If we want to undertake an expedition, then we first have to collect some information. We need a map and some knowledge about what we will need on that journey. The model of our 'psychical organism' is such a map.

Reflections and Discussion

■ All psychical forces are together in a manifold active relation. They influence each other, mostly without us realizing it. The wholeness of all psychical forces can be considered as a psychical system.

We designate this reality as the: 'PSYCHICAL ORGANISM'. We also use the term 'psychical-spiritual organism'.

What do you associate with that term?

■ The single psychical forces can be put together into 'classes' or 'sub-systems'. The different sub-systems are:

- Action (behavior) in the world (Psychology of behavior)
- Psycho-dynamism and its psychical energy
- The ego with its auxiliary functions (will, defense mechanism, integration, etc.)
- Intelligence (from the perception of thinking to learning; the cognitive psychology)
- Emotions and Feelings (the whole spectrum from love to hatred)
- Needs (psycho-physical, psychical)
- The unconscious (with the conscience)
- The 'spiritual intelligence' that operates in dreams, imagination and contemplation
- The force of love with all its performance potentials

Would you add a further system? Which?

■ The mutual influences of the singular psychical forces are manifold; some examples are given (you can add more):

- Feelings influence thinking
- Needs drive perception and actions
- Perception is influenced by wishes
- The unconscious acts on feelings and on thinking
- The capacity for love forms feelings and thoughts
- Dreams activate moods
- Psycho-dynamism is formed by thoughts and experiences
- Actions are produced by different inner psychical forces
- What we have in our consciousness, influences our self-being
- Suppression and oppression make our psychical energy tense

■ Some characteristics are:

- The psychical life is a complex and manifold inner reality.
- The 'psyche' is like the body an 'organic wholeness'.
- Each human being has a 'psychical organism'.

Note:

In general and primarily, we understand the 'unconscious' as 'the reservoir of experiences'. The unconscious is also an intelligent source of creative impulses.

Diagram 1.3: The Psychical Organism

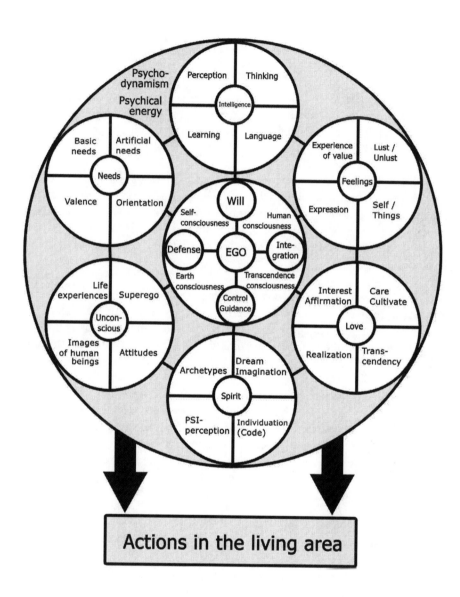

Comment: Instead of 'Intelligence' we can also say 'cognitive functions'. The 'EGO'-system presumes cognitive functions. But the main characteristic is the 'control-function or 'management-function'. Therefore we separate this psychical system from the cognitive functions and put the 'EGO-System apart.

The Neurotic Person

'Neurosis' basically means: an unconscious resistance against drive impulses and against the own potentials to live. Repressing the sexual desire produces a drive which piles up; its psychical energy must be discharged by means of a compensating (replaced) satisfaction.

Let's widen this orthodox psychoanalytical view: Neurosis is generally a denial to realize one's own evolutionary human being. A neurotic person rejects his psychical life, ignores his inner potentials (abilities, talents), and as a consequence declines his self-realization determined from his soul. First and foremost it is a resistance against becoming mature, leading to undesirable development.

This development causes inappropriate adaptations to the environment. Life converts into living replacements. Such a person lives in life lies. He avoids his self-being, blocks his authentic inner forces – e.g. love and inner needs – and reduces his existence and his genuine being to the remaining external and accepted possibilities.

On the one hand the psyche is separated in such an interaction to the world. The unconscious can act without limit; these are the complexes and the not cleared up life experiences. The inventory in the subconscious pushes the person to repeat earlier experienced, learnt and lived patterns. The freedom of choosing adequate patterns (of behavior) is significantly reduced.

On the other hand the interaction with the reality is confined within limits. The essential neglect to realize oneself genuinely produces compensatory needs. The world of the objects serves to satisfy lust, also to agitate the suppressed themes with its psychical energy (libido).

The suppressed themes (complexes, unsolved conflicts, denied potentials, etc.) convert into a powerful projection. Money and properties, power and lust for objects, often destruction and sadism, replace the genuine self-realization. The more a person is hindered from agitating these suppressed themes in such ways, the more the energy of the rejected themes causes psychical disorders or psycho-somatic reactions.

The consequences are: compulsion, anxiety, depression, etc., or often physical suffering, sometimes even cancer. Apart from that the character of such a person becomes rigid, inflexible, insensible, insensitive (or hyper-sensitive), unable to learn in all psychical areas.

At the end the person is left with guilt; and the neurotic person has to deny, even magically, this guilt on the realization of himself. This rejection acts with full power, with the sworn formula "the psychical life doesn't exist", often with a heavy suffering of the person or by others in his environment, manipulating them with his attitudes of denial. Anxiety is an after-effect.

The belief on the myth of the religious dogmas and its practice are also such a magical armor-plating of rejection.

Without a doubt one has to say that the American and European people are thoroughly infected with the contagious neurosis. The neurosis produces itself and binds all life as far it can't protect itself from this energetic influence. Every neurotic person is pushed to infect others with this 'neurosis'.

In the collective culmination phase a war always breaks out, so history teaches us. The neurosis – the life lie – is always a dead end, in which the suppressed collective life drive energy accumulates, until it can somehow breakthrough.

Narcissism as a Pattern for Perceiving Life

Narcissism is a type of neurosis; characteristics are: A self-image that is in the tendency grandiose, infantile, archaic and overvalued. Performances serve as a compensation for a weak ego. Performance tends to increase the ego and not the performance of a task. The world of the objects serves for the extension of the ego; this can be e.g. car, money, furniture, clothes, properties, and jewels. Other people are only perceived under the interest of a personal need / satisfaction; in that context they become objects.

The identification with a leader figures and the 'best of the world' in politics, economy, sport, show business, etc., serves for the extension of the ego. Narcissistic people admire and idealize top performers, the 'number 1', the best, the most powerful men, the most beautiful women, and the richest in the world, etc. An identification with a football club or other clubs with highest performance demands, with esoteric or religious communities also serve the extension of the ego.

The extension of the ego is also a fact in exaggerated self-perceptions and self-representations. Such an ego demonstrates itself on the one hand as big and strong, on the other hand is mostly weak and very vulnerable. Another indication for narcissism is an exaggerated and inappropriate intensity of care, protection, fusion, indirect control and a tendency for harmonizing with other people or groups.

The identification with objects, persons or institutions in most cases has an undertone of sexualizing an object or person (people) – as if it would have to do with sex or being enamored.

Furthermore we can acknowledge: a deficit of ability to accept anxiety, an insufficient drive control, inaccessibility as a mask, a deficient relation to reality (perception and dealing with), a lack of distance, partial self-indulgence, over idealizing father and mother and often teachers or priests. Finally we can identify narcissism behind an identification with a religion or a religious community that promises salvation but rejects that a person has to elaborate his salvations himself, e.g. with personality education and psychical-spiritual development (Individuation).

Causes are:

- A deficit of love, warmth, goodness and human attention during childhood
- A strong determination through others with rigid roles during the educational phase
- Repressing genital lust through educational norms and control
- Experiences of loneliness, abandonment, separation and exclusion
- A lack of positive appreciation as a person during childhood and youth
- A strong tendency to underestimate one's own values, forced through education
- Repression of feelings, of the problems with trust and dedication
- A very strong super-ego that forces suppression and with that to life lies
- Emotions of powerlessness and ego-weakness (etc.) caused by upbringing

Ways of resolving:

The more a person is ready to accept his psychical-spiritual organism (the psyche) and to understand it as his being, the more he is ready to form this psychical-spiritual organism to an all around balance.

Self-education and Individuation change the relation to oneself, to others, and to the elements of the real world, to God and religious institutions on earth.

Notes and Perspectives

What purpose does the psychical organism as a whole serve in daily life?

Write down the central keywords from this sub-chapter:

What does it mean for being a human when the psychical organism is the essential psychical-spiritual existence?

Explain: Knowledge about the psychical organism is important because…:

What do people learn about the psychical organism in their parent's home, at school and in the church?

What importance does the psychical organism have in the communication between life partners and in social interactions in general?

Which forces from the psychical organism do politics and the economy not consider?

What does advertising convey to us about the psychical organism?

Formulate some questions about the psychical organism:

1.4. Exercises

1. What are in our society in general the attitudes about the psychical life?
2. Which of the psychical forces do people hardly ever experience and not know much about?
3. Which psychical forces do people manage rather badly?

4. Self-knowledge - Self-image
4.a) What kind of human beings are my best friends? Spontaneously describe with 10 keywords:
4.b) What kind of human being are the majority of people in the Western society? Describe with 10 keywords:
4.c) Compare your notes in 4a) with 4b). Which aspects of view and judgment are especially striking?

5. Now repeat the same exercise 4a) and 4b), using the Diagram 1-3: 'The Psychical Organism' as an orientation:
5.a) What kind of human being are my best friends? Describe with 10 keywords:
5.b) What kind of human being are the majority of people in the Western society? Describe with 10 keywords a person you know:
5.c) Compare your notes in 5.a) with 5.b). Which aspects of view and judgment are especially striking?
5.d) Compare your notes in exercise 4.a) with 5.a). What are the predominant differences?
5.e) Compare your notes in exercise 4.b) with 5.b). What are the predominant differences?

What are your conclusions about the results from exercises 4 and 5?

6. Importance of Psychology in every day life.

■ To learn self-knowledge as a key-qualification

- To perceive the inner life differently
- To form the psychical forces systematically
- To use efficient methods competently
- To put the spiritual education in a network
- To build up a progressive holistic development
- How to systematically clear the biography
- Learning self-management for one's personal life
- Creating health and mental fitness
- Forming a relationship as a partnership
- Living sexuality with love and self-identity

■ It is useful to find distance in daily life, so you can concentrate on new forces. Give an example of importance:
■ Learning to manage and to reduce stress and burdens is part of self-education. Give an example of importance:
■ He who puts his feelings, his thoughts and his experiences of life in order, can find inner freedom. Give an example of importance:
■ It is sensible to learn, how to deal with conflicts and life. Give an example of importance:
■ Spiritual education is fruitful if it is networked with all psychical forces. Give an example of importance:
■ He who builds up step by step his capacity for love finds a deep meaning for his life and can work out and realize extensively his individual life-plan. Give an example of importance:

Multiple Choice Test

Choose the four correct answers and mark them with a cross like this: ☒ a) lust

1.1. The human being and his psychical life: Basic terms of the psychical life are:

- ☐ a) Force of love
- ☐ b) Pride
- ☐ c) Unconscious
- ☐ d) Needs
- ☐ e) Thinking
- ☐ f) Success

1.2. The manifold images about human beings: Psychical and spiritual aspects for consideration and reflection about human beings are:

- ☐ a) Depth psychology
- ☐ b) Pedagogy
- ☐ c) Brain physiology
- ☐ d) Philosophical-anthropological
- ☐ e) Ideological
- ☐ f) Social

1.3. The psychical organism as a model for an image of man: The model of the psychical organism renders possible the following statements:

- ☐ a) All psychical sub-systems work in interaction with each other
- ☐ b) The suppression of one of these sub-systems provokes undesirable developments in other sub-systems.
- ☐ c) Actions are connected with all psychical sub-systems.
- ☐ d) Harmony exists when in the whole psychical system all is transformed into spirit.
- ☐ e) Thinking functions most efficiently without love-feelings.
- ☐ f) All sub-systems are equal parts of the whole system.

2. Holistic Growth

An optimal multi-layered image of human beings is a pre-condition for progressive paths towards peace, fortune and meaning of life.

Essential Theses

❑ The psychical forces are formed through the whole life starting from the prenatal time.

❑ The result of this forming process can be manifold throughout the whole spectrum from positive to negative, from constructive to destructive, from suitable to unsuitable.

❑ The holistic image of human being is procedural, that means it also consists of the process of the psychical-spiritual evolution.

❑ Individuation is the psychical-spiritual process of development, growing with all the psychical sub-systems, in harmony with the internal and external world, especially also an expression of love, spirit and truthfulness.

❑ The holistic image of human beings consists of the whole spectrum of what is (actual state), what is possible and what can be achieved out of Individuation by determination and duty ('should be' state).

❑ The living space is part of this holistic image of the human being, as a real expression and a frame of condition.

2.1. Shaping the Psychical Forces

The human being is born into a life environment and from that moment begins to be formed and shaped. Already during the prenatal time the basic feelings of the mother and the relationship influence the psychical life of an unborn baby. The first psychical processes of growth are molded by the care and love from the mother, by the family relationships, by the style of upbringing from both the father and the mother, by brothers and sisters, and by people close around.

School then further educates and intensifies already formed psychical forces: abilities, behavior, conscience, thinking, feelings, self worth, needs and attitudes.

The child learns to perceive, talk, think and deal with things and people. From the earliest childhood everybody takes in eventful images about himself, about human beings and about life in general.

Many of these are probably unsuitable or even negative or harmful for future life. The unconscious becomes burdened with depressing experiences and strict norms. Deficiency of love and satisfied needs influence the will and self-management.

Already at an early age, the psycho-dynamism can be chronically tense and nervous or paralyzed.

Attitudes assimilated in earliest times later decisively influence thinking and behavior. Is there a lot of discussion in the surroundings? Is there a lot of stimulation and cooperation in the family? A child assimilates these communication patterns.

A child learns to see what the parents are seeing. The child learns how to reflect it thinking and decision making, as those do around it. The main elements of the consciousness are built up from the early school years.

If the parents care about their feelings and the feelings of the child, this child will also learn to care seriously about its feelings. If the parents discuss dreams and love, the child will assimilate these realities. If the child takes on an image of a 'punitive with a beard', under emotional music, then also here the basis of religious attitudes are formed.

The more these forming processes of education (shaping, forming, upbringing) are unsuitable for life, the more the person is forced to develop a compensatory behavior. This starts with the parents: Do they live with masks and façades?

If parents speak dishonestly with a lack of clarity and with constant compensations, then a child and an adolescent assimilate these life patterns: to put on masks, to enact trickery, to form symptoms and to live compensations. This can be defined as 'self-refusal'.

In a constructive case an adolescent learns direct and transparent behavior and a positive integration of the psychical life.

Progressive patterns for the mastering of life create and form 'competences' (skills) of living and allow for a self-realization.

Reflections and Discussion

■ From the prenatal time the psychical forces are formed through learning processes. During this process of development, these forces interplay in more and more complex ways. This happens through upbringing, school, and socialization (that means: assimilation of culture and cultural performances).

What is your first spontaneous thought to that?

■ From a certain perspective the human being is a 'product of learning'. Man is and lives what he has learnt. Everything that he learns and lives is based on the previously held learning processes.

■ We can manage our learning processes. We can correct, change, widen and deepen them.

What do you think about this, looking back at your biography?

■ We can consider the singular psychical forces, the sub-systems and the psychical organism as wholeness under the aspect of forming and educating.

We distinguish two processes of forming

Options of forming psychical functions:

● Negative forming:	● Positive forming:
▪ Inhibited, blocked to learning	▪ Open to learning
▪ Undifferentiated	▪ Differentiated
▪ Unconscious	▪ Conscious
▪ Disordered, chaotic	▪ Ordered, structured
▪ Not or badly controlled	▪ Controllable
▪ Unbalanced	▪ Balanced
▪ Unpredictable	▪ Predictable
▪ Destructive	▪ Constructive
▪ One-sided	▪ Manifold
▪ Suppressed	▪ Developed, considered
▪ Defensive	▪ Integrated

Which keywords are evocative for you?

■ The following characteristics are significant:

➔ The psychical forces are always the way they are formed and educated.
➔ There are different qualities of forming and educating processes.
➔ The forming and educating can take effect for or against man.
➔ Mankind has the possibility of influencing the process of forming and education.

Diagram 1.4: The Processes of Forming

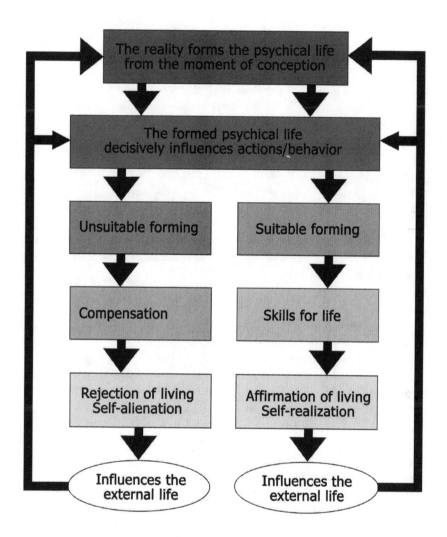

The reality forms the psychical life from the moment of conception

The formed psychical life decisively influences actions/behavior

Unsuitable forming

Suitable forming

Compensation

Skills for life

Rejection of living
Self-alienation

Affirmation of living
Self-realization

Influences the external life

Influences the external life

A Human can Change Himself

Psychoanalysis teaches that a person repeats, during his entire life, the patterns he learnt in his childhood, in most cases only with minor changes. Behavior psychologists say that we can change behavior and emotional reaction patterns. Indeed, a person can change himself from the foundation of his inner being; if he wants to, and performs what is necessary.

- A person can change his expectations relating to himself, others and the world; he can adjust his expectations more and more towards realistic possibilities.
- A person can change the image he has about himself in the same manner he truthfully perceives and develops himself.
- With self-education a person can realize his dispositions, talents and possibilities, as far as the frame of his life allows him.
- It is indeed possible to resolve conflicts with oneself, with the partner and with life in general. In this process the person also changes.
- A deeper satisfaction with oneself and with life in general is possible if the person learns to live more and more authentically with himself and together with others.
- Emotions that hinder changes – such as envy, greed, hate, self-doubt, etc. – can be resolved to make the process of change possible.
- A higher sincerity and honesty toward oneself is possible, if the person wants it. With that the process of changes starts.
- Rigid limitations, narrow attitudes and unbalanced beliefs can be dissolved (changed), in order for the psychical life to grow and develop.
- Ego-centrism, narcissism and false pride hinder changes, until the person is prepared to systematic and profoundly reflect.
- Accepting oneself more and more is a precondition for change. Accepting the individual being one is; is the beginning of every change.
- A person can reflect his exaggerated ideals and illusions about himself and about God and life. And with that one can change these ideals and illusions to authentic and realistic images.
- A critical reflection about the content of our consciousness (of what we have in our 'screen') about ourselves, others, life, transcendence) is the engine for change.
- The elaboration of the biography is the daily work of substantial changes that leads to a renewed being with inner freedom, dignity and humility.
- Destructive behavior is mostly influenced by the environment and by the subconscious of the person. Those that dedicate themselves to this reality will be able to change themselves.

- We can explore, elaborate and resolve even very difficult and muddled situations in the inner and external life with the purpose of producing changes.

Conclusion: A person can change himself and his life toward an increase in; sincerity, love, satisfaction, fulfillments, and happiness. But he must contribute by being willing and motivated. Valuable aims are not achievable if we do nothing. Changes of the psychical-spiritual being toward more and more quality lead at the same time to a genuine fulfillment of life. Everybody can activate hope, motivation and initiative. Each person has the freedom to choose living with life lies or in the truthfulness of the psychical-spiritual evolutionary human being.

- Our society has eliminated the social status as a determined condition and allows the rise into an upper class through individual performances and promotions.
- The determination – of what a person can become – is fixed neither by dispositions (inherited potentials) nor through environmental factors.
- The areas of life of a person are a result of work, interpretation and changes; therefore these areas are furthermore changeable with the person's changes.

Turning Point – The Beginning of Changes

- A person doesn't live from the dynamics of his drives and instincts. He has to form his drives and instincts, and he has to integrate them into his 'ego' control.
- The development of a person basically starts from his inner disposition and from his individual character. Self-determination is never outside of one's own inner being.
- A person becomes a person only through education and self-education. The freedom of choosing educational aims also demands self-responsibility.
- A person finds his own standards of values and a worthwhile aim of life in his own inner being; that means in his ability to develop his psychical organism.
- Finding a sense of meaning to life starts with discovering and forming one's own psychical organism. A genuine life meaning is never found without or outside this educational process.
- The fulfillment of life is given if a person has formed an all-sided balance in his psychical organism, and if he realizes from this inner state his life aims.

Turning points of change in one's own life:

The first turning point of change in life is the acknowledgement: "I have a psychical inner life."

The second big turning point of change results from a thorough self-contemplation: "I don't want to continue living the way I have lived up to today. I want to make more out of my life!"

The third big enlightenment arises after the first touching self-knowledge: "Now I have to work on myself during a long period of time so that a new life can grow."

That is the turning point of change for a new life!

So what does such a new life bring with it? A person for example, lives more and more his own life instead of the life pattern of others. One's own way of life and the whole dealing with life, results from the inside and are therefore a genuine expression of oneself. The self-esteem grows. The ego-strength reinforces itself from within. The self-image becomes more varied and the perception of others becomes more realistic.

It is obvious that such processes develop in small steps. That's the real authentic life!

In the 'new life', the psychical inner life gets organized. Thinking becomes clearer, more free and especially more creative. Frustrations and anger can be dealt with in an easier way. The capacity of assimilating becomes more efficient. The inner balance is easier to find, even during severe 'storms'.

The inner complexes that cause a depression or compulsion or anxiety or other disorders are reduced. Exploring one's own biography produces a cleaning process ('psycho-catharsis').

The result is more freedom and renewal in the inner life and in the external life. Psycho catharsis unleashes new energies for every daily life. Change through transformation becomes possible!

During these transformations one's own path of life becomes clear. One can then form new life perspectives. One's own realistic visions convert into a power of motives for creating new life projects.

New life knowledge increases, dormant dispositions come into development, and the life forces are strengthened. With a newly formed life culture one can realize one's own authentic human being.

After the middle of this working process comes another turning point of change:

- The person finds his inner center.

- The complete inner renewal is achieved.

- The hunger of the soul can be satisfied.

- The relation to one's own body and lust become positive and essentially life-affirming.

- A truthful love relationship is now possible. Interests, dispositions, needs and desires are all-sided balanced.

- The ego can manage the psychical life, and is supported by this inner life.

- One day at the goal of fulfillment, the person reaches the wholeness of his new being.

Notes and Perspectives

What purpose does the forming of the psychical life serve in daily life?

Write down the central keywords from this sub-chapter:

What is the human being without the conscious forming of the psychical life?

Explain: Forming the psychical life is important because…:

What did people learn about the forming of the psychical life in their parent's home, at school and in the church?

What importance does the forming of the psychical life have in the communication between life partners and in the interactions in general?

How do politics and the economy benefit from the forming of the psychical life of the human beings?

What does advertising convey to us about the forming of the psychical life?

Formulate an important question about the forming of the psychical life:

2.2. Individuation as an Evolutionary Process

Personality education starts with self-knowledge and leads to the forming process of all the so-called psychical forces in all sub-systems. This requires saying 'yes', respect and care.

With reason a human can discover his entire psychical life, can learn to understand it and, if needed to form it anew. At the same time he can consider all of the psychical forces and develop them to an all round balanced state.

During this process inner freedom and a more fully developed independence increases. So the psychical organism can work more and more as a unity and wholeness. Love, truthfulness and the principle of the inner Spirit in dreams and meditation support this process.

Through increasing processes of change and enlargements of the psychical possibilities a progressive dynamic arises. He, who consciously creates such a process and forms himself within that orientation, lives Individuation.

The so-called 'circle-cross-Mandala' is a symbolic representation of that process. We can simplistically interpret: The circle represents the wholeness. The vertical stands for the psychical-spiritual reality and the horizontal marks the terrestrial life. The cross goes beyond the whole, which we can interpret as 'realization on the earth'. The centre of the cross is the symbol of the spiritual principle.

This abstract structure is a so-called 'Archetype'. It represents the psychical-spiritual organism in the state of the performed process of Individuation.

At the same time this Archetype is an image of another transcendental reality in the spiritual world: God. We haven't "invented" this. This is an irrefutable fact, which anybody can experience in contemplation and dreams.

Individuation is only given, when psychical and spiritual self-education is connected all-round with all the psychical forces and when this is practiced with a clear expression in the external world.

The anti-model to the 'human being living in Individuation' is the 'archaic human being'.

The archaic human is characterized by rejection of the psychical life and by neglecting and deviating away from the psychical organism and by suppressing love and the spiritual intelligence. At the same time the archaic human is completely tied to his unconscious psychical life.

The consequences are: inner conflicts and disintegration, internal lack of freedom and infantile dependency. In every daily life such an uneducated and unformed psychical life is expressed by greed, envy, hatred, destruction, and a despotic and ego-centered drive. This human being neither has truthfulness nor solidarity for psychical-spiritual values of the circle-cross-Mandala.

Reflections and Discussion

■ There are numerous models for human development and growth. We can find them in:

▪ Psychology	▪ Pedagogy	▪ Philosophy
▪ Religion	▪ Esoterism	▪ Gnosis
▪ Mysticism	▪ Ideology	▪ Sects

■ We take care of our external appearance, create our living space, and develop and produce techniques for every day life and much more. We appreciate goods, we want technical perfection.

But how do we care for the forming of our psychical forces? How seriously do we take our psychical life? How do we develop our inner potentials? How do we live with our inner life and with them form the others?

Find some answers.

■ The psychical-spiritual process of development, called 'Individuation', is essential for the psychical organism.

This inner evolution is the process of becoming 'new', of a 'spiritual re-birth', of a psychical-spiritual transformation as we know it from mysticism and gnosis, of course in other terms and images.

Individuation allows for a 'catharsis' ('clearance') of the lived life back until the prenatal time, up to the integral personality. That means: the highest level of the psychical-spiritual human being.

What do you think about that?

■ Every genuine path to 'enlightenment' integrates the whole psychical organism and performs with the process of Individuation.

A genuine spirituality and a so-called 'higher consciousness' entail and require this process.

Holistic psychical and spiritual education of human beings requires the integration of all the realities:

- The psychical sub-systems with their singular psychical forces
- The process of Individuation as 'catharsis', education, development and growth
- Life spheres in which man lives, are formed and educated

What else does a holistic education demand?

■ The fundamental components that an all encompassing image of the human being has to contain, if the process of inner evolution shall guide to the highest aims, is herewith exposed.

Diagram 1.5: Evolutionary Human Being

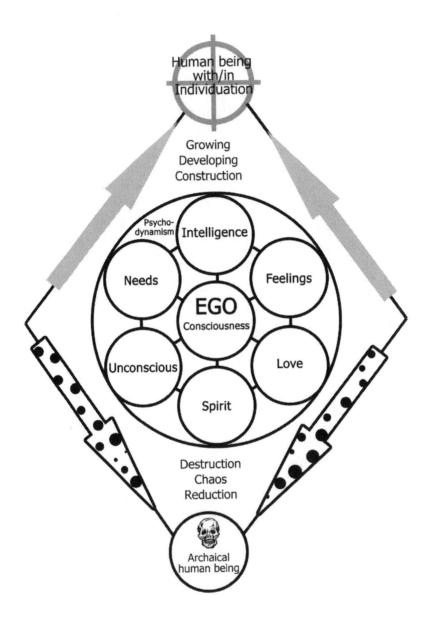

Development and Growth – Model of Steps

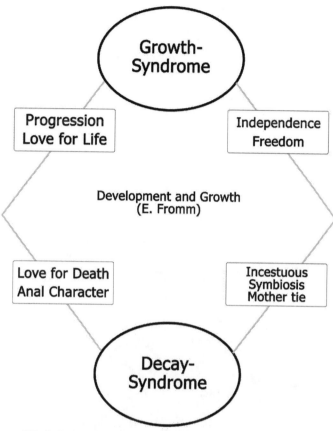

E.Fromm: Die Seele des Menschen (Stuttgart 1979)

'Development' means a steadily going higher and wider and with more and more flexible structures. Dynamic: each preceding step is the condition for the following step of development:

▪ Moral Judgment	▪ Parents-Children concept
▪ Understanding of justice	▪ Religious judgment
▪ Empathy	▪ Altruism
▪ Concept of community	▪ Concept of others
▪ Concept of intention	▪ Self-concept
▪ Concept of personhood	▪ Beliefs
▪ Concept of friendship	▪ Family relationship
▪ Concept of peer groups	▪ Overtaking of roles

A. Flammer: Entwicklungstheorien (Bern 1993)

Picture W1-51: Individuation in the symbolism of mandalas
The alchemistic presentation of the process of inner growth.
Jung, C.G.: Psychologie und Alchemie. Olten 1972
(1987), page 229; represented here as a geometric model:

"Opus"
The big work of Individuation

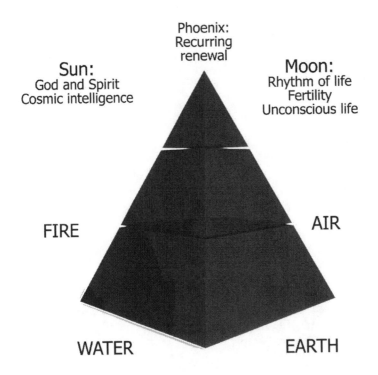

Phoenix:
Recurring
renewal

Sun:
God and Spirit
Cosmic intelligence

Moon:
Rhythm of life
Fertility
Unconscious life

FIRE

AIR

WATER

EARTH

Notes and Perspectives

What purpose does the evolutionary human being serve?

Write down the central keywords from this sub-chapter:

What is the human being without Individuation?

Explain: Individuation is important to people because...:

What did people learn about the evolutionary human being in your parent's home, at school and in the church?

What importance does the process of Individuation have in the communication between life partners and in the interactions in general?

How do politics and the economy use the potential of the evolutionary human being?

What does advertising convey to us about the evolutionary human being?

Formulate an important question about Individuation:

2.3. Humans' Realization in Life Fields

An image of human beings without a living space is something very abstract. We can't describe the psychical life without an environment.

- What is thinking without content?
- What is the unconscious without images?
- What is consciousness without assimilated realities?
- What is love without life?
- What is the psychical life - and with that the human being - without the terrestrial?

Any image of the human being obviously has to be put into the context of a real world. Only in the external reality can we extensively recognize and understand the human being.

Man creates his environment. Without creating a living space nobody can live. This is a specific ability, which no animal has in the same manner: In snow and ice, in the desert, in the virgin forest, everywhere man can create his living space. The inventive talent is nearly endless.

Today man can create technical support for everything. We make our food, our clothes, our living space, our means of transportation, our communication systems and much more.

We create institutions to organize our life in communities. We build up education systems to prepare the next generation for our way of life. All this and much more people around the world create and do in many different ways.

The creation is the environment in which everyone is born. What each of us in that world can become is influenced from this created environment. All the following generations inherit the creations. But living spaces and goods of our culture are made not only because of the necessity to survive.

We create a lot out of creativity, for lust and fun, for curiosity, for love, for joy and out of the drive from the unconscious life. A lot of our created world is a symbolic expression of the psychical forces and the inner images.

It appears that there are nearly no limits to what the human being can do and create. The human being can produce means of destruction. He can exploit the resources so that one day there will be no more.

What ever man does, it produces side effects, partly in nature, partly as a result of using the goods produced.

The created living space always also has repercussions on the psychical life and on the following generation. The psychical life is in a reciprocal action with the created environment.

If we want to understand the human being, we have to consider at the same time his living space.

The question forces itself upon the mind:

- Where should man limit himself?
- What is the sense of an infinite expansion?

If we connect this question with the psychical organism and the process of Individuation, we can find constructive answers.

Reflections and Discussion

■ We can't adequately comprehend the human being without his living space. Human beings are always in a system of time and space.

Every spiritual expression, what ever it may be, is connected with this terrestrial system. The psychical-spiritual evolution proceeds in a historically created situation.

How do you see that?

■ Individuation doesn't guide us away from the 'terrestrial life', even if introspection has temporary priority.

Individuation guides us into our living space and is a dynamic basis for the creation of our life.

Individuation shall find an expression in all life systems:

▪ Family	▪ Relationships	▪ Ethics
▪ Economy	▪ Industry	▪ Philosophy
▪ Social life	▪ Training	▪ Politics
▪ International life	▪ Intercultural life	▪ Services
▪ Work for peace	▪ Culture	▪ Education
▪ Religion	▪ Creation of areas	▪ Work

■ We can consider, analyze and judge the actions of man in the various life systems. Basic questions to that are:

- What is man doing?
- Why does man do that?
- How does man do that?
- Under which inner and external conditions does man do that?
- What biographical elements presuppose the actions?
- What is man doing that for?
- Which deeper sense can we recognize in the actions of mankind?
- Which deeper sense and which values are absent in his actions?
- How do his actions change, if his psychical system changes?
- How do his actions change, if the life space changes?

■ Mankind can recognize in himself how he is living and how he creates his living space.

■ Objects of our culture and relations between humans, in politics as well as in the neighborhood relations, are expressions of what an individual is as a psychical-spiritual existence, formed by his biography, shapeable in the present and in the future.

What do you think about that?

Diagram 1.6: The Network of the Human Being

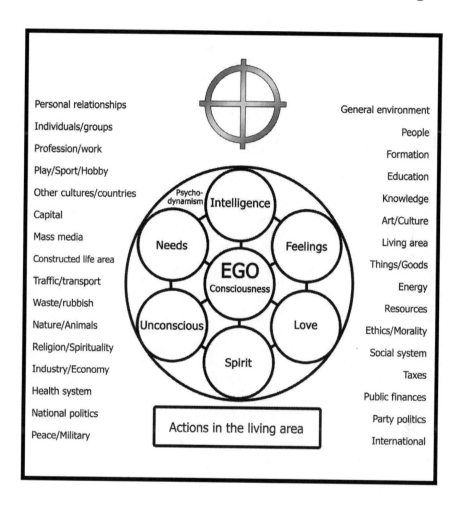

Personal relationships
Individuals/groups
Profession/work
Play/Sport/Hobby
Other cultures/countries
Capital
Mass media
Constructed life area
Traffic/transport
Waste/rubbish
Nature/Animals
Religion/Spirituality
Industry/Economy
Health system
National politics
Peace/Military

General environment
People
Formation
Education
Knowledge
Art/Culture
Living area
Things/Goods
Energy
Resources
Ethics/Morality
Social system
Taxes
Public finances
Party politics
International

Psycho-dynamism
Intelligence
Needs
Feelings
EGO
Consciousness
Unconscious
Love
Spirit

Actions in the living area

Environmental Adaptation and Self-Realization

The nature of the human being drives him to adapt to the environment and through that to realize himself. There are many ways that the human being can adapt to the environment. This is also always dependant on the quality of his psychical-spiritual forming processes and with that of his skills to act.

A. The anthropological-historical perspective:

1. To mark, to give names, to categorize, to value
2. Movements in and around the space; to explore, to investigate
3. Exploitation of nature for livelihood
4. Exploitation of nature for resources
5. Appropriation through domestication of animals
6. To appropriate through conquest and subjugation of other human beings
7. Appropriation of human made structures (constructions)
8. Appropriation through artistic and scientific representations of space
9. Appropriation through communication

B. The psychological perspective:

1. Motion and mobility: to touch, to grasp, to go, to sit, to drive
2. Exploration of the environment with feelings and senses
3. To manipulate, make, produce, categorize, form, develop, destroy
4. To dominate with mental capacities (e.g. language, calculation, measuring)
5. Communication: using space and objects for communications
6. Possessions, administration of nature and constructed areas:
    - Temporarily or permanently
    - Through occupation, seizure, marking, expropriation
    - Through fencing in and enclosing
    - Through defense, law and order
    - Through devastation (burnt soil)
    - Through legal or illegal occupation
    - Through violation (of laws, norms...)
    - Through buying, selling, renting
    - Through inheritance
7. Personalization of areas: furniture, decoration, to embellish with plants, to put up personal things, changing and remodeling, rebuilding and making the personal living environment cozy.

C. The responsibility for self-realization adapting environment:

1. Becoming a human being demands reflection about the way one deals with resources. Self-realization is a process between dealing with life issues and with one's self.

2. A person takes in possession environment and creates his life realities through his psychical dispositions. Environment and psyche are in an active mutual interplay.

3. The more a human understands his psychical reality and the interconnections with the life fields, the more he understands the products, the constructed environment and the world.

4. People dispose, administrate and manipulate their environment; dealing in such a way doesn't give them a chance to find their freedom.

5. Adapting environment always happens with communication. How do people speak if they are not fully aware of the way and effects of their environmental adaptation?

6. Creating a personal environment demands responsibility. Without responsibility a personal life environment remains an external purpose-oriented object-world, never a meaning-oriented opportunity (potential) and an expression of self-realization.

Psychical Functions and Criticalities in the World

Psychical-spiritual functions are the causal factors for criticalities in the world:

Write down some relevant psychical functions that cause a criticality:

1. Air (e.g. contamination):	
2. Population growth:	
3. Water:	
4. Soil:	
5. Plants (e.g. deforestation):	
6. Animals (e.g. mass-transport):	
7. Urbanization:	
8. Traffic:	

9. Electricity:	
10. Weapons:	
11. Food production:	
12. Waste/rubbish:	
13. Climate:	
14. Chemistry:	
15. Psychotropic medicine:	
16. Accidents:	
17. Alcohol:	
18. Food:	
19. Consumption of tobacco:	
20. Consumption of sweet things:	
21. Medicaments:	
22. Strength and power:	
23. Capital formation (e.g. fraud):	
24. Acquisition of goods (e.g. theft):	
25. Body and life:	
26. Expansion of living areas:	
27. Work:	
28. Information/Knowledge:	
29. Media:	
30. Health:	
31. Psychical life:	
32. Performances:	
33. Exploitation of working forces:	
34. Resources:	
35. Radioactivity:	

Notes and Perspectives

What purpose does the reflection about the interplay between life area and human being serve?

Write down the central keywords from this sub-chapter:

What is the human being without the reflected creation of living spaces (habitat)?

Explain: Reflecting the adaptation of the environment is important because...:

What did people learn about the interplay between human being and environment in your parent's home, at school and in the church?

What importance does the environment have in the communication between life partners and in the interactions in general?

How do politics and the economy deal with the environmental burdens?

What does advertising convey to us about the interplay between environment and human being?

Formulate an important question about the network between human being and environment:

2.4. Exercises

1. How do people experience and judge the development of their psychical forces?

2. Which of the psychical forces would you think that people especially should form, develop, strengthen and change?

3. Which images do people have about their possibilities of development? Describe with some short statements:

4. Give a spontaneous example to the following statements:

- People experience contradictions and opposites in their inner life:

- People are in their inner life basically fixed on:

- Peoples' psychical principles of control are:

- People experience their unconscious as:

- People guide and manage themselves in their everyday life:

- People should transform in their inner life, I think:

- In the last few years the following has changed with people:

- The relation of people to the opposite sex is:

- People could develop in their inner life:

- The psychical forces of people are in general:

5. The importance of the psychical life of the human beings means to me:

- People practice love in the following way:

- The following within people is not in harmony/balance:

- People experience their wholeness as:

- The comprehension/intellect and the feelings/needs of people are:

- People feel harmony between their inner and exterior life:

- People are reliable because their psychical life is:

- When people educate/form their psychical forces, they experience the result like this:

- People use intuition in the following way:

Your conclusions:

6. Write down the number that applies to a majority of people for each statement:

4 = People do it / live it / have it regularly
3 = People do it / live it / have it often
2 = People do it / live it / have it some times
1 = People do it / live it / have it a few
0 = People do it / live it / have it rarely/no

☐ People integrate their psychical life entirely.
☐ People are open to discover the realities and to see how they are.
☐ People live connected onto their inner process of development.
☐ People live with a high consciousness about their inner life.
☐ People care about orderliness and an equilibrated structure in their inner life.
☐ Dreams and meditation are a superior authority for people.
☐ People have a high level of inner freedom (unconscious, thinking, attitudes).
☐ People think, feel and mostly live constructively (realizing a 'tree of life').
☐ People experience themselves and their life entirely conscious.
☐ People expand their knowledge and abilities, their life in general, with quality.
☐ As far as people have power, they use it for promotion and guidance.
☐ People are positively dedicated / orientated to life with their whole being.

☐ The human bonds people have, live it progressively and constructively.

☐ People totally accept the psychical-spiritual life.

☐ People are open to learn about the psychical life.

☐ Peoples' inner life (unconscious) is easily controllable, predictable and balanced.

☐ The more people elaborate their biography, the more they feel a new life.

☐ The force of love is essential for people in everything they live, also professionally.

☐ People have clearly experienced inner transformation in small aspects of their life.

☐ The inner opposites in people's mind are increasingly dissolved to a balanced wholeness.

☐ People live in harmony between their inner life and their external life.

☐ People have experienced via meditation the meaning of the circle-cross-Mandala.

☐ The psychical forces of people are entirely and widely developed.

☐ People care about their feelings and needs.

☐ People come across all well formed psychical life with respect.

☐ People experience themselves as an inner unity.

☐ People confront themselves with transcendental dimensions with reason and realism.

☐ Truthfulness is something very important in people's life.

Total points: ....

Interpret the state and the tendency of people's regression-progression:

Determine some measures for a progressive development:

Multiple Choice Test

Choose the four correct answers and mark them with a cross: ⊠ a) lust

2.1. The forming (education) of the psychical forces: correct answers are:

☐ a) Learning processes start from the moment of preschool.
☐ b) A suitable forming guides towards life competences.
☐ c) Self-realization has got to do with the power of assertiveness.
☐ d) Man can change his earlier results of the processes of learning.
☐ e) Psychical forces can be formed negatively.
☐ f) Man can consciously contribute to determine his actual forming processes.

2.2. Characteristics for the psychical-spiritual development are:

☐ a) To release all 'terrestrial' needs
☐ b) Harmony between internal and external life
☐ c) Truthfulness
☐ d) Realization of the spiritual principles
☐ e) Ego-dissolving
☐ f) An all-sided connection of all psychical subsystems

2.3. The network of man in his living space: Individuation is particularly important in the following areas:

☐ a) Development of the psychical forces
☐ b) Relationships
☐ c) Guidance of people
☐ d) Acceptance in society
☐ e) Cultural life
☐ f) Mental-training

3. Personality Qualities

He, who looks after the aims of his self-education in the psychical organism and in the process of Individuation, can find a steady dynamic foundation for his life.

Essential Theses

❑ Educating means: well-aimed acquisition of knowledge, turning towards, recognizing, analyzing, defining goals/purposes, widening, changing, practicing, realizing, evaluating.

❑ The goals of personality education are based on the model of the psychical organism with the anthropological implications ('categories of education').

❑ Education aims always stand within the process of the psychical-spiritual development. They always refer to the reality of life.

❑ Goals of personality are also based on the interest of knowledge, action, growth and fortune.

❑ The formulating of purposes needs a clear understanding and judgment about dimensions like:

- Developed-undeveloped
- Conscious-unconscious
- Unfolded- not unfolded
- Ordered-chaotic
- Balanced-unbalanced
- Integrated-rejected

❑ The aims and purposes are based on interests like knowledge, growth, fortune and action; these are in turn aimed towards higher values and on basic life values.

❑ Ideals and values like 'happiness', 'peace', 'hope', 'joy', 'harmony', 'self-fulfillment' and many more can be discussed constructively, if they are bound back to the psychical system, in the process of Individuation and at the same time in the external reality of life.

3.1. Personality Education as a Process

Self-knowledge and Individuation find their concrete expression in personality education. 'Education' means: to form, to create, to change, to learn, to acquire and to grow.

Education is in that sense a working process with varying goals and methods in different areas. The areas are defined through the model of the psychical organism in the living environment.

The methods have different levels. Firstly one has to acquire a determined knowledge. The relevant knowledge (theory) has to be understood when integrating the concrete reality.

What we perceive in that action, we express through language. This includes also analyzing any given situation.

Each analysis of human facts reaches the history of development, which includes the dimension of time and space. After that we can define the aims of change, of widening and differentiation. This happens by coupling back with the inner spirit and with the force of love.

In order to create a manifold balance of the education processes, we have to link up the purposes in the context with other relevant psychical forces. Then the actual formation follows: state 'A' changes into state 'B' in the direction of the defined aims. The result can be realized in life. Finally we can examine what the application in life creates.

If we form all the psychical subsystems and the singular forces step by step, then they will have effects on many areas of life: The personal life will have a distinguished, manifold balanced character.

Certain disturbances will be solved through that education process automatically. Some problems won't even begin to turn up. Life challenges, crises and suffering can be mastered through self-education.

The general forming of one's personal life areas achieves an equilibrium, which is internally centered. Life areas will be created for the human being, and not for ideological or economical interests.

Just like man is trained to competently manage certain sectors of his life with abilities, from driving a car to professional talks, with personality education he acquires competences for life, to direct and use his psychical reality.

➜ Competences (knowledge and skills) for living change life.

Anyone who never learned to drive a car, but who drives nevertheless, produces damage and surely does not feel good about himself. With the psychical organism it is the same.

Those who can handle their psychical life, experience self-values, a built up self-confidence, and can find satisfaction, joy and happiness.

➜ Personality education is a requirement of life.

Reflections and Discussion

■ Education is an occupation with the following graduate processes:

▪ To acquire knowledge	▪ To care for the psychical reality
▪ To recognize singular elements	▪ To interpret perceived elements
▪ To analyze the contents of perception	▪ To understand historical aspects
▪ To define the goals of change	▪ To feed back with all forces
▪ To change circumstances	▪ To bring into play in life
▪ To evaluate success	

What do you understand by the term 'education'?

■ With this kind of education process of all psychical subsystems, we have connections between formation and results/effects:

▪ Creating the daily life	▪ Creation of the living space
▪ Difficulties in life	▪ Crisis
▪ Conflicts	▪ Disturbances
▪ Sufferings of life	

■ Education in that sense is not psychotherapy; conditions for psychotherapy are:

- Necessity for medical care
- Necessity for personal care
- Handicapped in the independent guidance of life
- Limitations in all kinds of living
- Incapability or reduced capability to work
- Actual suicidal tendencies

→ 'Problems are an indispensable part of life'. What do you think about that?

■ When the singular steps in that education process are taken as an inner experience the answers to the basic questions of existence manifest themselves, firstly and above all about the meaning of life and the values of being human.

Various general life themes receive a new depth:

▪ Fortune	▪ Peace	▪ Basic confidence in life
▪ Wisdom	▪ Joy	▪ Love
▪ Hope	▪ Self-confidence	

What do people wish in addition to that for their life?

What would people wish to change in their life?

Diagram 1.7: Forming the Psychical Organism

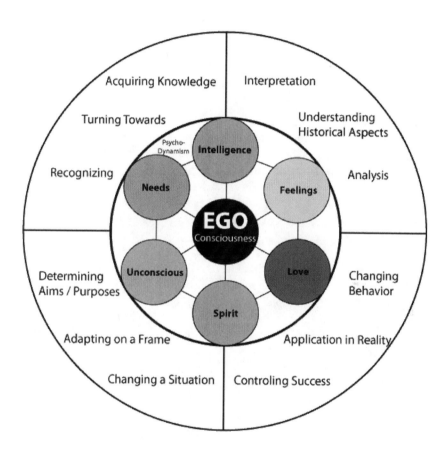

Learning 'Personality' or Educating 'Personality'

In everyday speech we understand 'personality' as a person with the following attributes: self-confident, self-dependent, determined, assertive, firm, decisive, etc. We define 'personality' as 'the individually formed psychical organism', continuously in a process of forming, developing, changing and differentiating. Personality is the totality of the psychological characteristics of a person.

Personality accentuates the individually formed and moldable totality of a person. If we talk about 'human education' (adult education) we extend the horizon with philosophical and anthropological dimensions. A man (person, human being) means in the core: the psychical-spiritual reality of all men (persons, human beings).

In another use of words, the term 'Self' means the same as 'person' or 'personality'. The 'Self' also has a spiritual dimension (C.G. Jung). Given that 'Self' first has a basic reflexive meaning and therefore means the whole person, we choose to talk about 'person', or 'personality'.

The basic thesis is: All psychical forces can be integrated fully into consciousness; these forces can be formed and changed consciously. Only very few people do this.

Most people don't even know that they could be responsible for their own self-education. They never learnt that this educational work is necessary for a constructive life. Many people even fear to come close to that psychical reality. They think that the subconscious is a 'black whole without bottom'. Or they think dreams are 'silly stories' and feelings (emotions) are annoying psychical forces.

Others say that love is sexual desire and satisfying needs. Or they believe that thinking works correctly automatically. But all this is completely wrong!

All psychical forces can be identified. All psychical forces can be taken into consciousness, can be reflected and changed. We can learn to manage all psychical forces in our daily life through integration into the 'ego-control'. Personality education is the key for success.

The way a person is formed psychologically, he lives himself, with others and with the environment. The way a person deals with his own psychical life is expressed in the way he treats the environment such as nature, water, air, world and animals.

A person creates his world in the same way as he is formed as a psychical-spiritual being. Personality education:

Forming Personality

- Personality education is the key-qualification for the personal and professional life.
- Personality education is in the future the indispensable part of all further education.
- Personality education creates the competences (skills) for constructive relationships.
- Personality education reduces many risks during life and in the social network.
- Personality education is useful; has manifold practical importance, stabilize self-identity.
- Personality education contains life knowledge and behavior, well reflected and elaborated.
- Personality education qualifies for leisure and for dealing with lifetime.
- Personality education produces inner security and trust into one's own forces.
- Personality education leads to an all-sided balanced well formed psychical organism.
- Personality education is necessary for an essential self-fulfillment during all life phases.
- Personality education integrates ethical responsibility for oneself, others, profession, society.
- Personality education is an investment for the future because the future will bring challenges.
- Personality education is a requisite for education, counseling, health care and management.
- Personality education reaches a person in his deepest psychical-spiritual being.

Our thesis: Personality education and Individuation form a type of person (human being), that in the future will be in demand in all systems of our society.

Educational Aims of Self-education

The 13 purposes of education of the healthy human being (Humanistic Psychology):

1. Widening perception of the reality.
2. Growing acceptance of oneself, of the others and the nature.
3. Increasing spontaneity.
4. Better focusing on problems.
5. More distance and longing for retreat.
6. Growing autonomy and resistance against acculturation.
7. Greater freshness of understanding, a greater richness of emotional reactions.
8. Higher frequency of transcendental experiences.
9. Growing identification with the human species.
10. Changed human relations.
11. Democratic character structure.
12. Strongly increasing creativity.
13. Certain changes in the value system.

Does a 'positive personal direction' exist as a self-dynamism of education?

The purpose, which each one would like to reach, the final aim, which he is pursuing knowingly or unknowingly, seems to be, to find him, to become himself. A realistic understanding of such aims requires taking into consideration some aspects and facts:

- A natural, not influenced and not disturbed development of a person doesn't exist.
- The psyche and the human behavior are in a complex and many-sided network
- Many forces which form a person stay out of his control.
- It is not true that a person wants to realize himself on a natural genuine way.
- A lot isn't as it appears; masks and façades cover many realities.
- Self-determination without knowledge and without working out experiences can not arise.
- To become free of the pressure of cultural norms implies the elaboration of this freedom.

Strong facts that express the demand of personality education:

→ Many people in our society suffer from depression and migraine, social phobias, chronic anxiety or insomnia; have daily headache, suffer from constipation, etc.
→ Many people in our society suffer from problems with their spinal column, or have allergies, chronic pain, asthma, heartburn, etc. Many people have thoughts about committing suicide.

→ Many people in our society are addicted: tobacco, alcohol, drugs, medicines, games, consumption, sweets, pornography, eating, watching TV, talking on the phone, etc.

- How many people in our society fail with their marriage?
- How many people in our society are cheating others?
- How many people in our society are victims of violence or economics?
- How many people in our society suffer from stress symptoms?
- How many people in our society live on the lowest economic level?
- How many people in our society suffer from noise emission (traffic)?
- How many people in our society live on social welfare?
- How many people in our society are unable to express themselves verbally?
- How many people in our society live alone and in loneliness?
- How many people in our society consume sex on the market?

→ Thesis: At least 50% of all these sufferings could be reduced through human education!

Notes and Perspectives

What purpose does personality education serve in everyday life?

Write down the central keywords from this sub-chapter:

What is the human being without personality education?

Explain: People's personality education is important because…:

What did people learn about self-education in their parent's home, at school and in the church?

What importance does personality education have in the communication between life partners and in the interactions in general?

Which kind of personality education do politics and the economy promote?

What does advertising convey to us about the necessity of personality education?

Formulate an important question about personality education:

3.2. The Formulation of Aims for Education

The result of personality education is to be classified neither as political, nor religious, nor esoteric nor spiritual. Nobody will become a racist, or a socialist, or a communist, or a Christian-socialist, or a Christian, or a Muslim, or a Hindu.

Individuation doesn't guide us to a determined psychological or philosophical position in the traditional manner. One doesn't become a disciple of a psychological-esoteric movement.

The whole theory, that means the psychical organism and the process of Individuation has a binding character; but the models are to be steadily revised, widened and formulated by science to become more practical. The concept developed and presented here is not about an 'idea' to be place beside a hundred other ideas and dogmas.

Personality education with self-knowledge and Individuation puts the human being in the centre of the aim. What each of us is with his psychical-spiritual reality and possibility is the starting point and the goal. Why should we define the goals outside of this existence?

In order for this education process to effective reach the entire psychical life, the aims need to be formulated in levels. As a criterion for orientation we have the psychical forces, the elements in living spaces (habitats) and the happenings of the education process.

Speaking about 'self-realization' in that context includes all psychical forces. He, who pleads for emancipation, is forced to describe this state with 'abilities to handle their own psychical forces'. Self-responsibility stands at the center of this psychical reality.

What does 'fortune' and 'success' mean, if it excludes the psychical reality? They turn out to be empty shells.

➜ Where does a personality education which trains only the intelligence and the ego lead to?

It is a field of activity for Pedagogy and Andragogy (theory of adult education) to research all the little steps of education (forming) of all psychical forces and to define them for an educational program. This can be discussed.

Nobody gives 'orders' here, nobody bans an 'apostate' and nobody forces others to pass over an idea. The goals and purposes of self-education are thematically clear and can be argued in stages. They always deal with growth, differentiation, development, harmonizing, flexibility and much more.

→ Thus we have end-goals which become new starting positions for new aims.

Life is always in motion. The psychical forces become a source for new creations. The living spaces with billions of human beings offer inexhaustible possibilities and challenges, to realize themselves and life.

Reflections and Discussion

■ The formulation of aims and purposes in the personality education is based on definite and essential foundations, which can be discussed:

- The psychical organism with all the psychical forces
- The process of Individuation
- The network with the life areas
- Steps in practical work of self-education

Until today how did you formulate your goals of education?

■ If goals of education are founded upon psychical reality and the life area, then we can operate with a clear understanding of the terms about the goals.

▪ Self-realization	▪ Emancipation	▪ Self-determination
▪ Self-actualization	▪ Self-responsibility	▪ Solidarity

Transform these goals into singular psychical forces!

■ Even general life ideals receive a clear foundation through formulation of aims and purposes:

▪ Happiness	▪ Fulfillment
▪ Success	▪ Joy

Describe such ideal goals in the context of the psychical forces!

■ Structurally, the end-goals all have the same basic components:

▪ Development	▪ Reinforcement	▪ Realization
▪ Growth	▪ Stability	▪ Creativity
▪ Differentiation	▪ Harmonization	▪ Clarity
▪ Balance	▪ Constructiveness	▪ Use
▪ Flexibility	▪ Availability	▪ Sustainability

What sounds attractive to you? Could you explain that?

■ All end-goals receive various grades in the process of education. In that sense it is suitable to say 'in the direction of... (End-goal)'.

Diagram 1.8: The Educated Personality

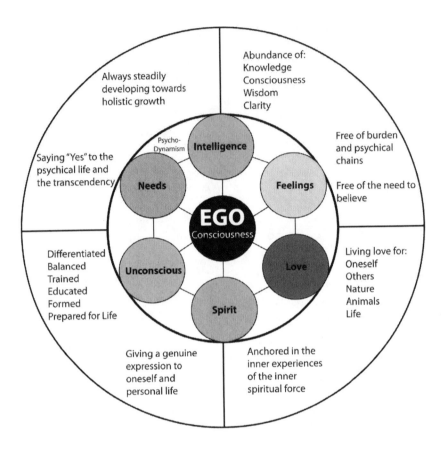

The Goals of Personality Education in Advertisements

Some examples (without references; the presented material is collected from the relevant press):

The way to sexual ecstasy	Increasing sexual lust
Awakening of dormant energies	The universal law to become rich
Personal success through intuition	To keep going endlessly
Get into the mood	Metaphysical healing
Being in love like a fish in the water	Successful career; to win
Trip into the multi-dimension	To be appreciated everywhere
Success with secret knowledge	Highest enlightenment
To have huge energy	Well-being and fitness to survive
To break limits	Spiritual therapy-technology
To become happy	The ultra fast path to spiritual bliss
To find peace with a smile	Experiencing the mysteries fast
Without health all is nothing	Experience the miracle in minutes
100 pages personality analysis for x €	To become wealthy and rich
Become rich fast with astrology	Experience the love of God
To enjoy life and to have fun	To be at one with the universe
To find acceptance, admiration	Healing through experience of reincarnation
Healing within 10 hours	Enlightenment through contacts with angels

Purposes of personality education from self-help books; some examples (shortened):

Speak and you will have success	Medicine against misfortune
Don't worry, just live	Become the N° 1
Live enthusiastically and win	Live positively
Each day a joyful day	Everyone can reach it
Believe in each other	There are solutions
I can if (when) I want to	Sunshine for each day
Tomorrow everything will change	How to manipulate coincidence
You are what you think	To live in harmony every day
Enjoy life; in spite of everything	Health above all
Recipe for happiness	He who is ill, is so by his own fault
See life positively	To be high-flyer

Our point of view about such educational promises:

They are rather deceiving and promise something that can't be reached; they encourage illusions; they are racial; they discriminate; they betray people that search; they simply lie; they exploit people who seek help; they keep those who seek the truth infantile; they are against depth psychology, against philosophical and sociological information. They are not acceptable from the point of view of the high human values of the pedagogical-philosophical thinking of the western tradition.

→ Form your own opinion, your judgments and reasons!

Alertness, Fairness and Sincere Criticism

Facts: Sects are criticized. Churches are criticized. Parties are criticized. Philosophies are criticized. Psychology is criticized. Science is criticized. Everyone criticizes everyone: the readers criticize the newspapers, the editors criticize the authors, the authors criticize the scientists, the scientists criticize the practitioners, etc. With good reasons we can assert: if Jesus Christ was alive again today, the majority of the editors, scientists, researchers, esoteric people, psychologists, priests, parapsychologists, politicians, and the 'normal' citizen (etc.) would (want to) crucify him again. Therefore, we sound a note of caution in all matters around 'the truth' and 'criticism'. It's difficult to correctly deal with people that say that they have the 'truth'; but it is also difficult to correctly deal with critics. The (mental, psychological, ideological, religious) location of both causes important subjective awareness! We generally suggest being cautious about 'truth' and criticism of those who declare to impart the 'truth'!

Sects offer human education. But what is a 'sect'? Is an educational institution with spiritual teaching and practices a sect? Why isn't the Catholic Church a sect? Are the free masons, or the Rosicrucian or the spiritual healer-groups also sects? A spiritualist may ask: Why isn't the community of education scientists a sect? Is it the teachings which characterize a sect? Or is it the way they do business? But, dubious business practices are found in all professional sectors and companies! Many motives drive people to organizations that the media and experts label as sects: the strive for affiliation, the search for wholeness, the need for a cultural identity, the need to be recognized or to be somebody special, the search for transcendence, the desire for spiritual guidance and the need for a vision.

There are many people that take part in esoteric and psychological organizations with the same motives. Yet these organizations are not called 'sects'. Where should a person go if he is searching for himself and for higher (spiritual) acknowledgement? What should he look at with critical judgment? The critical questions, which help us for a clear view about the values of human education and personality education, are simple:

- Are the psychical forces of the human being and the whole psychical organism entirely considered, taught, educated and changed (by these organizations)?
- Do the institutions/teachers practice the methods, which create a holistic self-knowledge, a self-renovation and a self-development for man and woman?
- Do they practice the inner way, guided and developed through the force of the inner spirit?
- Do they reach and form all those psychical forces in the human being, which cause problems, sufferings, damages and wars?
- Do they guide humans to the spiritual force, the source of life within each human being?
- Does everybody receive a deepened psychological consciousness about everything that they experience as 'religious'?
- Do they build up peace in the world, from the 'roots', namely in the unconscious psychical forces within the human being?
- Do the heads of educational institutions (organizations) reflect and form their own psychical organism and their acting, considering the deep psychological background?
- Do the heads of educational institutions (organizations) reflect upon the deep psychological effects of their power behavior on the unconscious life of everybody?
- Do they clarify the dynamic of projection and the way one can fix (bond) his libido on an institution, person and teaching?
- Do they love the human being with his psyche and do they love life as an expression of the psychical life?
- Do they promote autonomy, self-responsibility, individuality, critical thinking, and the archetypal processes (transformations) of the complete psychical life through Individuation?

Notes and Perspectives

What purpose does a model about the educated personality serve?

Write down the central keywords from this sub-chapter:

What is the human being without educational aims?

Explain: The formulation of educational aims is important because...:

What do people learn about educational aims in their parent's home, at school and in the church?

What importance do educational aims have in the communication between life partners and in the interactions in general?

Which psychical-spiritual educational aims show themselves in politics and the economy?

What does advertising convey to us about psychical-spiritual educational aims?

Formulate an important question about the formulation of educational aims:

3.3. The Justification of Goals

Everyone can refuse personality education and choose any system to master and create his life.

Everyone has the freedom to say: 'My feelings don't interest me', or 'love and spiritual intelligence are empty chatter', or 'my belief is my welfare', or 'my capital is my fortune'.

Primordially it is a subject for everyone to examine and decide if and how extensively he wants to educate himself.

As long as the damage in society as a result of uneducated people is tolerable, personality education won't be practiced extensively.

But if the lack of self-education guides us to catastrophic conditions in our state, to a general destruction of the environment, then mankind will start to discuss whether to practice self-education or accept the risks.

The discussion about the justification starts with the decision whether we have an interest in what each of us has as his own psychical life and how this reality influences our actions and life existence.

If we recognize how the created living space depends on the formed psychical forces, how there is a coherence between lack of love and suffering in life, how an unmanaged unconscious life binds each of us, then we start to be interested in growth.

You want to educate yourself, to develop yourself, to form yourself and to evolve in your life. You want to create culture and not destruction, peace and not war, justice and not injustice, love and not hatred, joy and not misery.

When the damages become dramatic, when people are killed around the world, when famine and misery put millions into a catastrophe, when the basic vital conditions of life are destroyed making millions ill with fatal effects, then everybody will begin to speak about whether enough reason exists for self-education, for a human environment, for relations with love and spirit.

The justification for personality education starts with a basic decision and then guides to the singular subjects of psychical sub-systems and the real life. Scientific research will constantly present new material that can be discussed.

Everyone can decide for himself, if and which purposes he wants to reach with self-education.

If the well-being of a state, of a continental community is seriously threatened, then we need personalities who will democratically put forward, and with the power of authority, self-education with love and spirit for our society.

The main life question that touches each of us:

→ Do we want to live? Do we say 'yes' to our life?

Reflections and Discussion

■ The context of justification lies in the basic principles of the goals, (of the psychical organism and the Individuation).

There is no need for some other system of ideas like philosophy, religion or ideology to find a relevant understanding.

Or, can you find some other context of justification?

■ A basic problem still remains: Each person can refuse such goals. The decisive preconditions lie in four areas of interest. Do people want:

■ Knowledge	■ Growth
■ Action	■ Fortune (self-fulfillment)

What happens if somebody does not have any of these interests?

a) Interest for knowledge:

■ Curiosity, lust of discovering	■ Desire to understand
■ Need for consciousness	■ Reflection about life experiences

b) Interest for growth:

■ To develop	■ To grow
■ To integrate (assimilate)	■ To live evolutionarily

c) Interest for actions:

▪ Drive to perform	▪ Drive to create (creativity)
▪ To widen living conditions	▪ To use the potentials of life

d) Interest for fortune:

▪ Meaning and self-fulfillment	▪ To live love and spirit
▪ Well-being	▪ Peace

■ The decisive basics to define and to justify the goals and aims (purposes) are:

➔ The increasing destruction of the environment and of human beings, a kind of principle of evolution: selection of the non-educated man

➔ The free will to a binding obligation based on the experiences of the psychical organism, especially the force of love and spirit (also reason)

➔ The four interests, depending on education; given that: the more the regression and the archaic state prevails, the more these interests are reduced

Do you see more essential basics to justify the purposes?

Diagram 1.9: Formulation of Aims of Personality

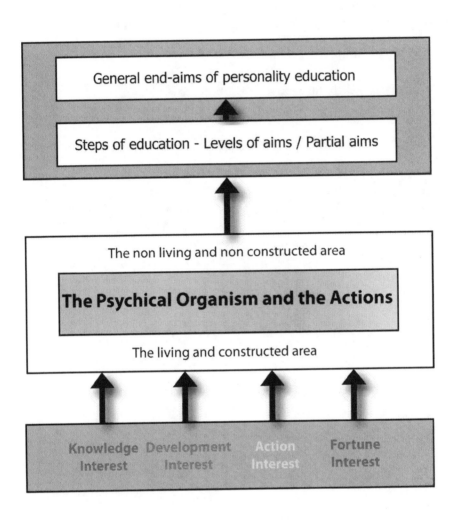

General end-aims of personality education

Steps of education - Levels of aims / Partial aims

The non living and non constructed area

The Psychical Organism and the Actions

The living and constructed area

Knowledge Interest   Development Interest   Action Interest   Fortune Interest

Goals of Learning in Personality Education

Every educational (pedagogic) process is orientated towards learning aims, which can be reached by teaching. The pedagogical theory distinguishes between aims of direction, rough and fine aims:

a) Aims of direction: becoming a strong and balanced personality; a complete self-realization; able to work under stress; to live a co-operative relationship; able to live a satisfying sexuality; realizing one's own potentials, etc.

b) Rough aims: Being aware, knowing and understanding one's own personality aspects; recognizing stress factors and being able to deal with them; strengthening the psychodynamic; knowing the principles of a partnership; able to talk with the partner, etc.

c) Specific aims: to integrate shadows; to analyze situations critically; learning methods of relaxation; acquiring communication rules; getting to know one's own potential; understanding the body language; able to talk about very intimate matters with the partner, etc.

Learning aims are distinguished in subjects, to whom they relate (in the pedagogical tradition): affective (feelings), cognitive (thinking) and psycho-motor (abilities) subjects of learning purposes.

General (formal) aspects when formulating purposes are:

- knowledge, information, recognition, consciousness, description
- being able, practicing, realizing, acting, reacting
- planning, coming into a new being, organizing, coordinating
- giving value, judging, giving meaning, understanding reasoning
- getting used to, training, adapting, controlling
- the network, structure, interrelation-system, surrounding system of a subject

Questions about the aim (purpose, goal; in life, of life) always lead to the highest aims:

- Possible highest aims of personality education
- Personality (as an aim)
- Moral character
- Democratic character
- Humanistic / Christian / socialistic personality
- Humanitarianism / Humanity

- Conscience
- Freedom
- Being aware of responsibility
- Self-determination
- Self-realization
- Love
- Virtue

The Philosophical Foundation of Aims of Education

Thesis: The foundation of aims basically lies in the ethics which is part of the Philosophical Anthropology, which means: founded in human images.

Those that seek educational aims, think philosophically, explore, ask questions and strive to understand themselves. Because the education of the human being reaches the genuine being and herewith also the genuine aims:

What can and should everybody hope for? What is the value of human life today? Following some suggestions from various books:

- Not to increase the possession of a Philosophy, but to deepen the philosophic thinking as a movement.
- The course of unstoppable progress is unstoppable regression; freedom in society cannot be separated from rational thinking.
- All that is rationalized is derailed; the single man is devalued, separated from spirituality.
- Rationality is the starting point of freeing the human being from his self-immaturity of his own fault.
- Fortune, health, justice, peace, freedom, maturity imply an imperative moment.
- 'Emancipation' will free from non-rational and unidentified compulsions.
- An act of self-reflection that changes our life is a movement of emancipation.
- Freedom is an ultimate cause, which can't be reduced to another cause. Freedom of the human being isn't any unlimited freedom, but an autonomous freedom, which itself gives it its laws.
- Without an obligation to laws, values, basic values of the human being, freedom is an illusion.
- A declaration and a kind of living in love, truth, consciousness, individuality, freedom, subjectivity can't be proven by the exact sciences.
- Each one has to learn, to give him a base for hope.
- Pedagogy (human education) has to set standards if it should help anyone to reach a behavior which is distinguished from fixed rails and built in

deviations, which is free from routes and roles of routes with constructed substituted routes, (and shouldn't) end in indifferentism, anarchy, skepticism, nihilism, criticism.

- Human education means: the first and foremost task to let a human being develop.
- The truly free human being wants what he can and does what he likes.
- Our entire wisdom consists of servile prejudice.
- The light of reasoning is given to us from God; the human being is released by a bond to God.
- The divine light is the origin of ability for knowledge and its capacity for understanding.
- Man doesn't know the real existence, and doesn't know about his ignorance.
- The human being is, because of his undeniable principle spirituality, an existence which can decide freely and which is open to act. He is obliged to create himself in his decision and acting, thinking and willing in order to create his world and to prove his spirituality in all his thinking and acting processes.
- Personal morality can't be formed out of an action itself, but only from the quality of the underlying will.

Notes and Perspectives

What purpose does the justification of educational aims serve?

Write down the central keywords from this sub-chapter:

What is the human being without a reflected justification of educational aims?

Explain: Justification of educational aims is important because…:

What did people learn about justification of educational aims in their parent's home, at school and in the church?

What importance does the justification of educational aims have in the communication between life partners and in the interactions in general?

How do politics and the economy justify the general educational aims?

What kind of arguments does advertising convey to us about personality education?

Formulate an important question about the justification of educational aims:

3.4. Exercises

1. What are until today your personality ideals?

2. How do you see yours 'unsuitably formed' psychical forces?

3. How do you see your 'suitably formed' psychical forces?

4. Develop one thought to the following questions:

- What happens when people do not care about their psycho-dynamic?

- What happens when people do not take their basic psychical needs seriously?

- What consequences arise when people let emotions go without control?

- What remains when people do not live their love capacity anymore?

- Where does it lead when people do not sufficiently use their intelligence?

- What can people expect if they never elaborate their unconscious life?

- What is the quality of the people's life if they live without meditation, dreams and the inner Spirit?

- What are the long term effects when people do not take their psychical forces seriously?

- What is a love relationship without conscious integration of the psychical life?

- What is the difference in people's life with and without their psychical-spiritual development?

5. a) Formulate three especially important aims of people's personality education:

5. b) What happens in people's life if they do not aspire to those aims?

6. Circle the formal aspects of aims which are especially important to people:

❂ Development	❂ Growing	❂ Strengthening	❂ Knowledge
❂ Distinction	❂ Flexibility	❂ Harmonizing	❂ Controlling
❂ Balance	❂ Capacity	❂ Availability	❂ Consciousness
❂ Freedom	❂ Creativity	❂ Constructive	❂ Order
❂ Usage	❂ Application	❂ Utilizing	❂ Integration

7. The educational question: What would you like to form new and to promote for people? Formulate a concrete aim considering the following points:

● Knowledge ● Capacity ● Organizing ● Judging ● Training ● Networking

Concrete initial aspect: Psychical force, personality aspect Chose an element:	Concrete aim: Describe the concrete aspect of behavior Formulate your aim:

Multiple Choice Test

Choose the four correct answers and mark them with a cross: ☒ a) lust

3.1. Personality education as a process: active educational performances to the psychical organism are:

- ☐ a) Not to take the past seriously
- ☐ b) Recognizing
- ☐ c) Understanding
- ☐ d) Domination of the unconscious
- ☐ e) to evaluate the result
- ☐ f) Acquiring knowledge

3.2. The formulation of educational aims: The following statements to the topic are right and suitable for the individuation:

- ☐ a) Purposes nearly always contain also an aspect of growth.
- ☐ b) Goals of personality education have to be bounded back to an ideology.
- ☐ c) The dogmatic belief as a base for deciding purposes is essential.
- ☐ d) The formulation of goals is always based on the psychical organism.
- ☐ e) End-goals and goals of processes can be dismantled into small aims.
- ☐ f) The network with the life area is an essential aspect of the formulation of aims.

3.3. The foundation of aims: The justification and foundation of aims shall contain:

- ☐ a) Interest for knowledge
- ☐ b) Interest to act
- ☐ c) Interest for growth
- ☐ d) Peak experiences
- ☐ e) Interest in fortune
- ☐ f) Interest for the 'Zeitgeist'

4. Self-knowledge as a Process

Systematic self-knowledge is a precondition for a human being-centered life and for an all around balanced development of life.

Essential Theses

❑   In general most people don't know or are only vaguely aware of about 1-5 % of their psychical life

❑   Most people refuse a deepened self-knowledge. They don't want to see and they don't want to experience, what they are in their inner life. They have never had a chance to learn that.

❑ Self-knowledge is the base and the essential precondition for a conscious and differentiated human being with love and spirit.

❑   Man can only guide, change, educate, form, develop and love what he knows and experiences inside as a reality.

❑ Self-knowledge reduces disturbances and difficulties, supports growth and development, frees from illusion and dependencies, activates responsibility and with that a consciousness about duty for oneself and for one's life potentials.

❑   Self-knowledge is a process:

● More and more knowledge: recognize and experience
● More and more actions: educate, develop, widen
● More and more fortune and self-fulfillment: realize and experience
● And then: more consciousness for more knowledge

4.1. The Openness for Self-knowledge

Self-knowledge is the starting point of every evolutionary way of life. Without self-knowledge the human being remains an 'archaic being', trapped in unconsciousness and inner chaos.

Most people don't know what to do with their dreams. Beyond certain psychological schools, publicity and political manipulation, the unconscious hasn't got any practical significance. Nobody is interested in it. Everyone 'somehow' tries to cope with their feelings and needs.

Only very few people make an effort towards methodical relaxation; most they rarely even question the level of their tensions.

Not many occupy themselves with how they perceive, think and speak. That people reject and suppress is rarely noticed.

The entire psychical life is only taught in fragmented pieces in primary education. Life will be the 'school' for adults, so they say. In life one learns: greed and envy, hatred and aggression, lies and masquerades, running the gauntlet and power strategies.

The one, who doesn't want to know anything about 'Psychology' and 'Personality Education', will hardly find access to self-knowledge.

The standard reactions are:

'I know myself well enough', or 'I am already developed', or 'nobody has got to tell anything to me', or 'I have had enough teaching', or 'it is written in the Bible, how human beings have to live', or 'I believe in God, that's enough', or 'I am modest and don't want any wisdom', or 'stop bothering me with that rubbish', or 'Being rich, one lives easier'. Again and again people have all kinds of reactions to the subject 'self-knowledge'.

If financial problems start in the married life, love and spirit quickly go away. For millions of people life is a fight for economic survival. What will self-knowledge achieve here? Solidarity for self-knowledge rarely exists in our society.

One can't earn money with self-knowledge, can't gain prestige, and self-knowledge hardly produces lust. The positive possibilities of self-knowledge are unknown.

Self-knowledge is a directed process of self-education. Man has to want that education. He has to learn certain methods. He has to do a series of clearly defined tasks. For that also some constructive attitudes are needed.

Those seeking self-knowledge, do so if they can see a gain in it – external, internal or spiritual. The one, who practices self-knowledge, appreciates higher inner values. The one who values his life higher than gadgets, goods or money, can build up an interest in his inner life.

→ Self-knowledge is an inner experience and not just cheap blabber.
→ How can you study Psychology and ignore the relevance for you?

Reflections and Discussion

■ Generally people don't know (or only vaguely) more than 5% of their psychical forces. Most have a very small consciousness about the effects of their psychical life. This has different reasons:

- Public schools teach little insight into the inner life and about the mode of action of the psychical life.
- The style of life in industrialized societies is oriented towards external values.
- The mode of thinking and the 'Zeitgeist' tends towards suppression of suffering, weakness, fear, feelings of inferiority, troubles and burdens.
- The bonding to material goods, to ideologies and dogmas is easier than working towards self-knowledge.
- There is an unspoken solidarity between people, which says:

→ Never find yourself!
→ Never look into your depth!
→ Don't take love too seriously!
→ Never reveal the life-lies!
→ Never tell the truth!

How do people see their consciousness about the effects of their own psychical forces?

■ Openness for self-knowledge is based on attitudes about life, such as:

- The inner experience is more important than words.
- Inner values stand above external values.
- Life stands above technology and industrialized organization.
- Self-education during the whole life is a way of life.
- Looking for orientation and stability in the inner life offers more security than external fixations.
- A manifold balanced life produces more self-fulfillment than living one-sidedly.

What about people's openness?

■ Hindering efforts to self-knowledge are:

- Suppressing feelings
- External hyperactivities
- Seeing problems and difficulties as 'negative'
- Fundamental thinking
- Rejecting everything related to psychology with prejudices
- Denying love and spirit as essential values of life
- Speaking more than thinking, and rarely reflecting on your own thinking
- Acting as if you know enough about human beings

Diagram 1.10: The Experience of Self-knowledge

SELF-RESPONSIBILITY
READINESS TO LEARN
SERIOUSNESS
HUMANITY
SELF-CONFIDENCE
ENRICHMENT
RECONCILIATION
RELIEF
OPENNESS
SOBRIETY
HONESTY
GENUINENESS
REALISM
OBJECTIVITY

Definition of Self-knowledge

Knowledge is aimed at one's own ego. The self as a created and durable concept in the experience of man is investigated under the perspective of its characteristics (own being, behavior, talents, abilities, attitudes, motivation) ...

Self-knowledge, as a precondition for development and creation of one's own personality was even demanded as a basis by the Greeks in the classical antiquity, as it can be recognized by the inscription on the temple of Apollo in Delphi: 'know thyself'. Self-knowledge, becoming aware of one's self, is based on the one hand on self-perception, on the other hand on sensation, which are taken from the confrontation of man with problems in his environment and the interpersonal communication... In spite of the legitimate demand for self-knowledge (Pascal, Kant) skeptical voices facing such demands were never lacking (Goethe, Nietzsche), which point out the tendency of man, also to mask himself.

To know one self ... (is) according to Socrates a precondition of morality. Lessing refers to it as the central point of all human wisdom; Kant said: it is the starting point of human wisdom. Wilhelm Meister wrote: How can one recognize oneself? Never through contemplation, but through acting one does recognize himself. Try to do your duty and you know immediately, what is inside you.

To know oneself was understood by the Socratic-platonic Philosophy as follows: that the human being must ask what is behind the sensual subjects of his knowledge, and must become aware of the preconditions of the ideas, mainly the idea about what is good. Also in the aristocratic Philosophy the man can only come to a right appreciation of himself, when he understands himself as the mediator between animal and God... What the human being is, he only experiences through the truth... The deepest (and highest) meaning of every self realization is ultimately also the recognition of God. Through that God becomes a personal part of the human being.

Self-knowledge contains:

1. Self-consciousness
2. Self-reflection
3. Knowledge about one's own real life (in contrast to self-fraud)
4. Knowledge about one's own existence
5. Knowledge about the true aim of one's life; or the reason that such an aim doesn't exist but only the absurd

➔ What the human being is, only his own history can tell him.

If the human on the street starts to get to know himself, if he thinks about his behavior, his morals, his feelings, the basis of his principles and his expectations... then he does nothing else than what a scientist does who investigates human behavior - only unprofessionally and unsystematically... If the layman could proceed scientifically, if he could only adapt the elementary bases of the science, then his chances to self-knowledge would increase considerably.

A human being is a creature, which harbors in himself the possibility, to sink to the level of an animal, or to swing onto a saintly life... the thinking, the consciousness, the being responsible makes the dignity of each human being.

Who am I? What am I? Perspectives in Everyday Life

- in the evening in front of the television
- after an opulent meal, two glasses of wine and a cognac
- on the beach, in the middle of masses of people
- after a working day, driving home, stuck in a traffic jam
- experiencing a drastic failure at work
- as a boss, dealing with psychically weak employees
- shopping in the supermarket, when very hungry
- during a heavy bout of flu
- after six hours walking, quite exhausted
- at a dinner, which comes too late and which is also too salty
- communicating with a psychologist
- when laughing
- in a moment of deep sadness
- being full of despair and helpless
- in a situation of deep humiliation
- when totally alone and can barely take it anymore
- when surrounded by meanness and intrigues
- alone on a Saturday evening with the need for tenderness and sex
- with friends and acquaintances at a party at 03.45 in the morning
- being with pets
- in the middle of a long period of unemployment
- after losing one's own business or a top-job
- a hard blow from destiny as a victim of a criminal act
- having made serious errors and recognizing that
- after losing one's life partner, a child, a good friend
- during a tedious period of stress

The self-image (self-identity): If people talk about self-image, they mean in general the totality of a person (the whole personality), the psychical life and the character, also the realized life potentials. The 'Self' is thus in the core the psychical structure, which means the psychical organism with all actions (behavior).

The self-image is the result of one's own self-knowledge. In the self-image a person constructs in the essence with a varied fantasy his own value, based on the superficial external being; oriented in the zeitgeist: money, properties, reputation, power, status, clothes, consumption, etc. One's own esteem is not based on the own potentials, talents, dispositions and skills; not on creativity, mind capacities, abilities to love, etc.

The self-image (and together with that the self-knowledge) is mostly an expression of adapting and self-denial.

The realistic self-image is based on:

▪ Wanting to widen the self-image	▪ Taking responsibility for one's own 'destiny'
▪ Acquiring knowledge	▪ Giving the necessary importance to the psychical life
▪ Consciously recognizing feelings	▪ Willing to learn and preparedness for self-education
▪ Flexibility in social adaptation	▪ Openness for a self-critical perception
▪ Exploring and elaborating rejected matters	▪ Practicing contemplation as a method
▪ Clarifying the content of the subconscious	▪ Wanting development and growth

Notes and Perspectives

What is the general benefit of self-knowledge?

Write down the central keywords from this sub-chapter:

What is the human being without self-knowledge?

Explain: People's self-knowledge is important because...:

What did people learn about self-knowledge in their parent's home, at school and in the church?

What importance does self-knowledge have in the communication between life partners and in the interactions in general?

How do the people in politics and the economy practice their own self-knowledge?

What does advertising convey to us about self-knowledge?

Formulate an important question about self-knowledge:

4.2. Self-knowledge as a Process

Knowledge in the mind about human beings doesn't create self-knowledge. Only the eventful inner experience of knowledge through the encounter with oneself can be defined as self-knowledge.

Therefore self-knowledge is not simply a subject of psychology, but more of pedagogy (adult education), the science of adult education.

Eventful self-knowledge places a complex manifold course into gear. Someone who consciously experiences the state and the functions of his psychical forces develops a need for change there where it seems necessary.

The more man recognizes himself, the more he widens his perception of others. He sees other people more and more differentiated.

Self-knowledge again and again guides us to the basic question: Why is that so? How did it become like that? This pushes us to an accepting and reconciling attitude towards our-selves and our biography. This is then the basis for meeting others.

The next step is to follow the first little changes in our own psychical life. This process influences our life style. That means movement, differentiation and more and more conscious self-guidance. These developments are seized by self-knowledge, from which we reach a wider consciousness about ourselves and life. The process is like a spiral.

Someone who grows through self-knowledge in this self-education process will also experience the influences in his relationship. He will recognize his life partner as differentiated as he sees himself. He promotes the development of his partner as he promotes his own development. He will come into communication with the inner experiences.

With that interchange about self-encounter a relationship becomes more and more dynamic. The dreams of the partner, the elaboration of the past life and the discovery of the genuine needs make the relationship creative and exciting. This is truthful love.

→ Without self-knowledge love cannot exist.

The utopia:

All adults train their self-knowledge daily for half an hour. The experiences are discussed at the work place on Monday as the main subject instead of extreme performances in sport. People tell each other how relaxation training works, how mental-training makes them free, to which interesting and exciting new discoveries the treatment of one's biography leads. 'Tricks' and 'knacks' in dealing with oneself are revealed and discussed. Instead of gossiping about the neighbor or curiously participating in the suffering of others, one speaks about oneself. Instead of chatting about money and career, fashion and cars, the human becomes the subject, the suppressed inner being, which can finally emerge.

→ This real utopia will probably very soon emerge as the only chance for a future.

Reflections and Discussion

■ Self-knowledge is a spiral process:

- The more man knows about himself, the more he understands his life.
- The more man knows about himself, the more he understands others.
- The more he understands himself and his life, the more he can grow.
- The more man grows, the more he can let others grow.
- Growth leads to more consciousness about oneself and about others.
- The widened consciousness is the starting position for further self-knowledge.
- The process of recognizing and learning goes ahead constructively.

■ Self-knowledge as an increasing process of growth and learning has an effect on the personal living space:

- Others are seen and experienced more differentiated.
- Relationships (intimate and loose ones) become clearer and deeper.
- Personal mobility becomes more conscious and more reasonable.
- Consumption becomes more conscious and more differentiated.
- Care for the environment becomes more reflected.
- Goods become instruments for life (and not the reverse).

■ Self-knowledge changes the self-relation, relationships with others and life styles. This is again a new frame for further steps of development in self-knowledge:

- A deepened experience of self-relation increases the benchmark for personal relationships and relationships in general.
- The deepened experience of relations promotes further differentiated self-knowledge.
- The more the life area, goods and mobility are consciously experienced; the more a new existential experience forms, if the human being stands in the centre.

■ The one, who takes self-knowledge seriously, also takes love and spirit seriously. Self-knowledge becomes self-love and love for life with spirit:

- Self-knowledge, love and spirit are closely connected and affect each other.
- We can't love anything that we don't recognize and don't want to care about.
- We can't love ourselves, but not life and being human.
- We can't live love and Spirit, and at the same time hate and destroy.

Diagram 1.11: Self-knowledge as a Spiral Process

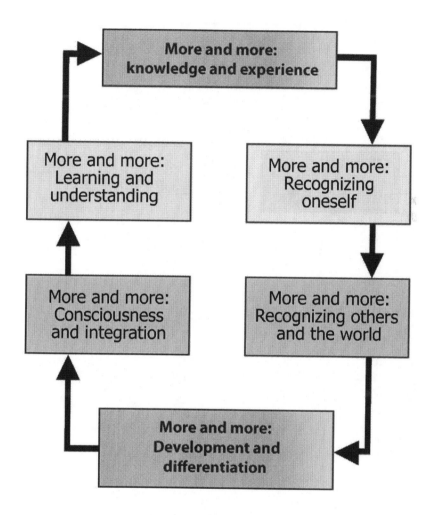

Progressive Dynamic of Taking the Personal Selfhood Seriously

Imagine: People take the following personality aspects seriously. What kind of consequences would they experience in their life?

Mood swings:	
Sociability:	
Cheerfulness:	
Passion:	
Restlessness:	
Feeling of inferiority:	
Vivacity:	
Nervousness:	
Excitability:	
Sensitivity:	
Ego-strength:	
Tendency to dominate:	
Joy for expressions:	
Super-ego-strength:	
Social courage:	
Suspicion/distrust:	
Being carefree:	
Keen perception:	
Tendency to feelings of guilt:	
Independence:	
Power to assert:	
Agreeable nature:	
Emotional instability:	
Helpfulness:	
Being unhappy:	

Need for acceptance:	
Self-confidence:	
Masculinity/femininity:	
Coolness:	
Objectivity:	
Nonchalance:	
Shyness:	
Thoughtfulness:	

Regressive Dynamic of Not Taking the Personal Selfhood Seriously

Imagine: People don't take the following personality aspects seriously. What kind of consequences would that have in their life?

Mood swings:	
Sociability:	
Cheerfulness:	
Passion:	
Restlessness:	
Feeling of inferiority:	
Vivacity:	
Nervousness:	
Excitability:	
Sensitivity:	
Ego-strength:	
Tendency to dominate:	
Joy for expressions:	
Super-ego-strength:	
Social courage:	

Suspicion/distrust:	
Being carefree:	
Keen perception:	
Tendency to feelings of guilt:	
Independence:	
Power to assert:	
Agreeable nature:	
Emotional instability:	
Helpfulness:	
Being unhappy:	
Need for acceptance:	
Self-confidence:	
Masculinity/femininity:	
Coolness:	
Objectivity:	
Nonchalance:	
Shyness:	
Thoughtfulness:	

Notes and Perspectives

What purpose does 'more and more knowledge' about oneself serve?

Write down the central keywords from this sub-chapter:

What is the human being without development, differentiation, growth and deepness?

Explain: Taking the personal selfhood seriously should be important to people because...:

What did people learn about the process of self-knowledge in their parent's home, at school and in the church?

What importance does the progressive dynamism of taking the personal selfhood seriously have in the communication between life partners?

How do politics and the economy take the progressive dynamism of personal selfhood seriously?

What does advertising convey to us about taking the personal selfhood seriously?

Formulate an important question about self-knowledge as a process:

4.3. Self-knowledge as Opportunity

Self-knowledge is the life opportunity for all men because the process that sets into gear is progressive, constructive and evolutionary. With education of the psychical forces many risks of life are reduced to a minimum.

Life always conceals risks. But many people guide themselves with their unconsciousness and their chaotic inner world, with high probability toward certain suffering and conflicts.

The pressure of the unconscious inventory alone already creates a large scale of destructive potential which in most people one day breaks through.

Also collectively we have to expect the consequences. The force of the suppressed unconscious (that means the unconscious inventory which is not integrated in the consciousness) is always stronger than the conscious ego with its will to reject and suppress.

In the collective there is no way to get out of that compensatory dynamism. The power play in the psychical life of the individual has to be considered in the network with the collective. Risks and opportunities reach everyone.

The individual becomes free from illusions and wrong ideas, of psychical dependencies and lack of sense. The more man proceeds with that education process, the less he wants to go back to an unconscious way of living.

Assimilated attitudes and beliefs are difficult to free, because they are often not identifiable as subjective ideas. With all their power they want to be realized.

It is liberating, if one reaches to break through them and find more valuable and much more appropriate beliefs deep within the inner life. This gives life many new forces and animates development.

The quality of the personal life improves, because human values start to work like engines in relationships, at work and in leisure time. Life can be lived completely orientated to real existence, and nevertheless anchored in transcendence.

If many people live their personality education, we achieve decisive, collective opportunities.

With this education the whole humanity opens itself up to a totally new path for the future. Let's imagine: In all countries everybody forms himself through this process of Individuation.

Politicians, philosophers, scientists, priests, generals, managers, teachers and many more start, to 'look into their own mirror', so that they grow into that process, where love and spirit can be developed. More and more men in power in the states and in the churches come to decisions founded on their inner spirit. More and more they draw up programs for an environment and a living environment with Individuation.

→ Can we assume that mankind will go on such an evolutionary path?

Reflections and Discussion

■ Self-knowledge is the starting point of all opportunities in our life, given that:

- The less man knows himself; the more he is dominated by his psychical life.
- The less man overcomes this domination; the more he is also dominated by his external reality of life.
- The less man knows himself and also others, the more he is vulnerable to lies, masks and façades.
- The less man knows himself and doesn't want to know himself; the more he can be manipulated by those who know how to use these mechanisms.
- The less man knows himself and his psychical life in general, the more he becomes a slave of mythology, ideology, dogmas and fundamentalism.

■ Self-knowledge is the basis for:

- Reduction of disturbances, difficulties, problems, suffering
- Support of relationships, love for human beings, wisdom, and love for life
- Stimulation of responsibility, development, growth, creativity
- Liberation from illusions, unrealistic ideals, fictions
- Humane handling of nature and sources of life

■ The spiral process of self-knowledge guides towards the transformation of Individuation, from the first stage to the second stage.

■ Every normally talented, ordinarily trained man with a serious interest in self-knowledge and human values of love can grow through self-knowledge until half way to the Individuation process. After that further efforts are necessary.

Growing through self-knowledge brings people:

- much less crime
- much more regard for life and goods
- much fewer accidents
- much more care for life
- much less social suffering
- much more support for self-support
- much less psycho-somatic disease
- many more healthy people
- much fewer children with disturbances
- many more happy/healthy people
- much fewer suffering elderly people
- many more fulfilled elderly people

Diagram 1.12: The Effects of Self-knowledge

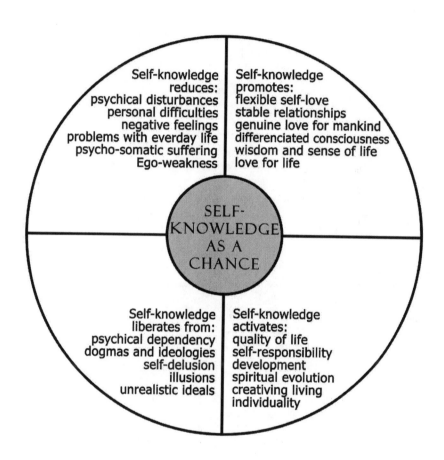

Self-knowledge reduces:
psychical disturbances
personal difficulties
negative feelings
problems with everday life
psycho-somatic suffering
Ego-weakness

Self-knowledge promotes:
flexible self-love
stable relationships
genuine love for mankind
differenciated consciousness
wisdom and sense of life
love for life

SELF-KNOWLEDGE AS A CHANCE

Self-knowledge liberates from:
psychical dependency
dogmas and ideologies
self-delusion
illusions
unrealistic ideals

Self-knowledge activates:
quality of life
self-responsibility
development
spiritual evolution
creativing living
individuality

Sociological Questions to Self-knowledge and Self-reflection

Judge your opportunities of self-knowledge. Imagine, somebody says to all the following statements 'these don't interest me', and somebody else says 'these questions give me opportunities'.

Mark those items, to which you can say 'this is critical for everybody'.

- [ ] I am always very content with my life.
- [ ] I am for a hard enforcement of all laws...
- [ ] I easily have stage fright at certain events...
- [ ] I find talking about general life questions only slightly interesting
- [ ] I am always in a good mood.
- [ ] Sometimes I would just want to daydream.
- [ ] We cannot blame somebody for exploiting somebody else...
- [ ] Sometimes I am thoroughly tired of everything.
- [ ] Sometimes I doubt myself.
- [ ] I am sometimes discontent with my personal situation.
- [ ] Many of my plans have failed...
- [ ] In reality my environment has nothing new to offer me.
- [ ] Often I miss somebody who puts his arms around my shoulders.
- [ ] My mood changes quite often.
- [ ] I have a deeply rooted feeling of being a valuable human being.
- [ ] It angers me, if any unexpected things disturb my daily course.
- [ ] Sometimes I have thoughts which embarrass me.
- [ ] There are times when I feel all empty and desolate.
- [ ] Often I need some more tenderness.
- [ ] My belief in God helps me.
- [ ] I do many things which I regret afterwards.
- [ ] There are moments when I need more self-esteem.
- [ ] My current life is going according to plan.
- [ ] I am often a bit clumsy in dealing with others
- [ ] Often I feel miserable without any recognizable reason.
- [ ] I like my life especially when something is constantly happening.
- [ ] Deep inside I sometimes feel loneliness.
- [ ] It regularly happens that I am discontent with myself.
- [ ] I am rather reserved and a bit shy.
- [ ] I constantly need new stimulations.
- [ ] I often say untruths.
- [ ] Sometimes I feel as if a strange power possesses my thoughts.
- [ ] Sometimes I feel a bit bored.
- [ ] I am often pensive about my past life.
- [ ] I feel rather sure, that I have good attributes.

- [ ] I am frequently searching for special experiences...
- [ ] A lot of my life is determined by destiny...
- [ ] I am somebody who tries to get to the bottom of all things.
- [ ] I sometimes have the feeling that all things are only an appearance.
- [ ] Sometimes I would like to have such an exciting life as other people have.
- [ ] I believe in the existence of a higher being.
- [ ] I have the feeling that I can be proud of a lot of what I am.

Self-Contemplation

Sit in front of a mirror, look into it and contemplate your face. What do your eyes tell you? And what does your mouth tell you? Contemplate yourself completely naked in front of a mirror and feel: Do you like yourself? And then, explore a bit around your life: What do you want to change? What should you do? Think about your future: What are you seeking? What do you want to achieve in your life?

And finally have a look through your past: Let your life go through your mind in a short overview, until your early childhood. How do you feel with your biography? What do you feel about your past?

Go through a spectrum about everyday life: shopping, cooking, house-work, body care, creating your living environment, eating, drinking, smoking, etc. Secondly go through your leisure time: watching TV, reading, making music, listening to music, doing handicrafts, painting, gardening, going to the cinema or theatre, surfing the internet or chatting, doing some sport, walking around, writing your dairy, interpreting your dreams, meditating.

Some activities you would like to do with others, with your life partner or friend, and with good colleagues: How is it with lust, tenderness and sex?

Have a look at the following list and search for needs: serious conversations, discussing conflicts, listening, participating, helping, giving great pleasure to somebody, entering into a dialogue, showing interest, and exchanging life experiences.

What can't you do? What do you absolutely not like? Maybe now you want to change or to tackle something. Or do you want to come to realize one day in the future when you are old, that you didn't live your life and yourself?

Self-contemplation means to bethink oneself: Who am I really? What do I live for? How do I live? Do I live myself or have I lost myself?

He, who can never contemplate himself, loses himself in the movements of life. He is manipulated, indoctrinated and enslaved. He doesn't live himself; he lives a given pattern.

He lives driven by the lust principle: lust with the medium of money, recognition, success, reputation and power. He is chained to that. That's the principle of the 'carrot and stick'. Self-contemplation also means: finding one's own meaning of life.

Can a person find his genuine meaning of life if he is living in life lies, if he is ensnared in neurosis and narcissism?

Can a person be free if his way of thinking is not free, if his subconscious dominates his emotions and daily behavior?

Can a person find his genuine meaning of life if he lives in mechanisms of defense and projection?

Some questions for a systematic self-contemplation

- Do people practice well-aimed methods for relaxation?
- Do people know a meditative technique to strengthen their life energy?
- Do people reflect their state of psychical energy?
- Do people meditate about their daily way of living?
- Do people contemplate about how they are?
- Do people understand their feelings, its causes and effects?
- Is it important for people to reconcile part painful experiences?
- Do people take their physical state (e.g. afflictions) seriously?
- Do people know their genuine inner needs?
- Have people already meditated about their projections?
- Do people know the way they deny (ignore) their inner life?
- Have people ever searched within for the so called 'the inner Spirit'?
- Do people practice self-management bonded in their inner life?
- Do people meditatively deal with their conscious and form it?
- Have people worked out their life experiences with meditation?

Notes and Perspectives

What are the opportunities of self-knowledge in everyday life?

Write down the central keywords from this sub-chapter:

What is the human being who rejects all essential sense of self-knowledge?

Explain: The opportunities of self-knowledge are important to people because…:

What did people learn about the opportunities of self-knowledge in their parent's home, at school and in the church?

What importance do the opportunities of self-knowledge have in the communication between life partners and in the interactions in general?

How do politics and the economy handle the opportunities of self-knowledge?

What does advertising convey to us about the opportunities of self-knowledge?

Formulate an important question about the opportunities of self-knowledge:

4.4. Exercises

1. What does the word 'self-knowledge' evoke?

2. Who/What are people essentially? Draw five aspects about people with some keywords:

3. How do people's acquaintances react to the request 'know yourself!'?

4. What concrete meaning and values do people give today to self-knowledge?

5. Why do so many people reject self-knowledge?

6. The profile characteristics ('entire tendencies of a person') of a majority of people are:

Mark: 3 = very positive/distinct 2 = moderate positive/prominent   1 = weak positive/distinct

☐ Firmness   ☐ Integrity
☐ Self-consciousness   ☐ Self-confidence
☐ Strong will   ☐ Health
☐ Self-identity   ☐ Holistic self-experience

- Performance ability
- Free of fear/anxiety
- Open to learn
- Self-management
- Self-contentedness
- Vegetative stability
- Willingness to perform
- Maturity
- Competences
- Energy, vitality
- Patience
- Willingness to compromise
- Relatedness
- Satisfied sexuality
- Living situation
- Talents
- Fulfillment of sense
- Sociable
- Taking responsibility
- Ability to suffer

- 'Style'
- Acceptation of life
- Flexibility
- Being adaptable
- Endurance
- Self-motivation
- Personal aura
- Determination
- Emotional stability
- Openness
- Readiness to help
- Able to deal with tension
- Happiness about life
- Stimulating Hobbies
- Ideal of life
- Life planning
- Moral Character
- Ability to roles
- Control of situation
- Body relation

Total points: .....

General evaluation:

Which of the profile aspects find expression in their working?

Which of the profile aspects do you see positive, constructive and with success for a personal life?

How can people support and strengthen their weakness of their profile aspects?

7. The daily life as a self-expression. Mark what affects you:

- ☐ Irregular daily rhythm
- ☐ Noise in the environment
- ☐ Watching a lot of TV
- ☐ No work contentment
- ☐ Negative inner bond with parents
- ☐ Guilty feelings
- ☐ Existential fear
- ☐ Unsatisfied sexuality
- ☐ A non elaborated passed suffering
- ☐ No professional future
- ☐ Unstable life partner
- ☐ Stress at work
- ☐ Concern about the own children
- ☐ No spirituality
- ☐ A lot of sad memories
- ☐ No/not enough love experiences
- ☐ No aim for life
- ☐ Drive of perfectionism
- ☐ Mistrust
- ☐ Forced to play a 'theatre'
- ☐ No co-operation in the relationship
- ☐ No basic confidence in life
- ☐ No own clear values of life
- ☐ Fear of big challenges
- ☐ Fear of unemployment
- ☐ Ignoring one's own problems
- ☐ Suppressing annoyance and anger
- ☐ Always putting aside own interests
- ☐ No time and no calm to eat
- ☐ No inner orientation (dreams)
- ☐ No constructive mastering of suffering
- ☐ A predominant rigid psycho-dynamism
- ☐ Low tolerance of frustration
- ☐ Frequently overstraining yourself
- ☐ Easily influenced in the mood
- ☐ Unilateral image of the opposite sex
- ☐ Only small experiences of faithfulness
- ☐ Not reconciled abortion
- ☐ Unsatisfied wishes
- ☐ Not enough movement (sport)
- ☐ Strong inhibitions
- ☐ No regular work
- ☐ No satisfied relationship
- ☐ Unelaborated biography
- ☐ Fear of life
- ☐ A disorganized life
- ☐ Tensions in the relationship
- ☐ Financial problems
- ☐ Conflicts of separation/bonds
- ☐ Lack of self-confidence
- ☐ Frustration in the housework
- ☐ Boringness in leisure time
- ☐ Lack of profound sense of life
- ☐ Unable to say "no"
- ☐ Strong religious norms
- ☐ Strong old-fashioned norms
- ☐ A lot of frustrations
- ☐ Lies of the people
- ☐ Delicate sexual experiences
- ☐ Unable to enjoy lust
- ☐ Unable to laugh
- ☐ Bad feelings about the neighbor
- ☐ Negative attitude about the body
- ☐ Discontent with living condition
- ☐ Strong need for harmony
- ☐ Unable to be alone with myself
- ☐ Exaggerated hindsight
- ☐ Ignoring the own feelings
- ☐ No clear and real self-image
- ☐ Diffuse and weak will power
- ☐ Fear of illness
- ☐ Lack of inner flexibility
- ☐ Doing too much that others say
- ☐ Drive for consumption
- ☐ Jealousy (own, from the partner)
- ☐ Repressed sexuality
- ☐ Ignoring responsibility for life
- ☐ Little personal autonomy

- ☐ No profound (self-) reflections
- ☐ Discord with others
- ☐ Constant grief
- ☐ Excessive hunger for experiences
- ☐ Unable to live authentically
- ☐ A lot of failure
- ☐ Low stable self-esteem
- ☐ Not enough inner distance

Multiple Choice Test

Choose the four correct answers and mark them with a cross: ☒ a) lust

4.1. Openness for self-knowledge as a personal experience: self-knowledge means:

☐ a) Becoming free of vice
☐ b) Inner enrichment
☐ c) Value independence
☐ d) Genuineness
☐ e) Realism
☐ f) Seriousness

4.2. Self-knowledge as a process: Characteristics for the process of self-knowledge are:

☐ a) The more man knows about himself, the more his life becomes confused.
☐ b) Others are perceived with more differentiation.
☐ c) Care for the environment becomes more reflected.
☐ d) The more man understands himself, the more he understands others.
☐ e) Self-knowledge frees us from terrestrial needs.
☐ f) Increasing self-knowledge generally supports learning processes.

4.3. The self-knowledge as an opportunity: With the time self-knowledge creates:

☐ a) Reduction of diseases
☐ b) Reduction of accidents
☐ c) Prestige
☐ d) Wisdom
☐ e) Liberation from illusions
☐ f) Total spiritualization of life

5. Methods for Living

Thorough personality education and far-reaching Individuation are the comprehensible paths to the mystery of 'being human'.

Essential Theses

❑ Practical personality education contains:

● Acquiring knowledge and experiencing it on oneself
● Techniques for relaxation
● Mental-training
● Dream interpretation
● Meditation: imagination/contemplation
● Rational-reflective systematic elaboration

❑ Self-education means: to live with learning, experiencing, forming, practicing, exercising, evaluating.

❑ The preconditions for personality education include a frame of life:

● Way of living with time and space
● Relationships for interchanges
● Motivation and clear steps to that purpose

❑ Self-education demands some basic attitudes such as: love, saying 'yes' to life, responsibility, solidarity, duty. Given that the rejection of self-knowledge and Individuation leads to the suppressed and uneducated (unformed) inner life expressing itself in other destructive forms.

❑ Many groups of people are excluded from the social life because of their specific weakness. That is the result of the lack of self-education.

5.1. The Practical Methods

Personality education is pursued with clearly defined methods. A little bit of sentimental self-experience and discussion don't activate the process. Without a deepened knowledge the efforts don't go far either. To read a lot about the psychical life is a must.

Thinking is an essential part of the work for self-education. The reflection about words used, the differentiation between emotional judgment and objective statements also is part of that. Thinking as fruitful work doesn't just 'happen like that'. One has to sit down for it.

A working diary is a helpful instrument. With that we can write down what we are thinking, and we can carry the thoughts towards purposes.

We can tackle each psychical subsystem with different methods. Some methods complement each other; they highlight various aspects. Meditation with the visualization of inner images is a basic technique.

This can be divided into different methods:

With imagination in general we can work out nearly all kinds of subjects. Contemplation helps to experience symbols and archetypes, which represent psychical-spiritual processes. Mental-training (with given inner key-images) helps to control our thinking, to free thoughts, and to concentrate with a fresh memory.

Introspection is more aimed towards inner sentiments: emotions, inspiration, self-experience and light psycho-somatic reactions.

Dream interpretation is essential to reveal the depth of the psychical life.

The intellect can never know which themes and inner changes are due to be worked out at a given time. It is similar to the growth of the body: If the ego could guide the body growth, very funny creations would grow up. Only the inner Spirit has the overview. In this spiritual intelligence – an intelligent inner force – is the code of Individuation.

We can also say: This inner Spirit sees and knows everything (a lot), retrospectively and prospectively.

There are more methods, which also complement the basic method for creative work, for example role playing, painting and creative body expression (e.g. dance).

In different cultures various methods may be practiced or at least practiced in different ways and styles of handling. Some may favor rituals. Others prefer more objective and sober working methods.

Many like to work alone, meanwhile others need the support of a group.

→ The manifold methods to make a living are part of culture.

Reflections and Discussion

■ The personality education, from self-knowledge to Individuation, contains different methods, which are variously dependent on psychical subsystems:

- 'Autogenous' training, progressive muscle relaxation, mental-training for: psycho-dynamism, psycho-physical relaxation, psycho-hygiene
- Practical imagination: visualizing inner images, contemplation for: all psychical subsystems, other people, institutions, for symbols and archetypes
- Dream interpretation: to interpret dreams, to widen with role plays or drawing for: all psychical subsystems, other people, institutions, human evolution
- Introspection: to feel for the inner life, to listen to oneself, to experience looking inwards: for all psychical subsystems
- Rational-analytical reflections: thinking, to work out with thinking: all psychical sub-systems, for clearing one's own biography
- To acquire knowledge: reading, autodidactic learning, training (courses) for: all psychical subsystems, other people, institutions, life in general
- To keep a working diary, a working book about the subjects and methods: as a support for orientation and systematize by all methods

■ The different methods complement each other. The imagination for example guides us to other aspects than thinking. The imagination and dreams serve to enter into the unconscious life.

The result has to be revised with thinking. Simply having inner experiences is not sufficient for changes, growth and expansion. Relaxation on its own doesn't establish personality education.

■ Learning the methods goes hand in hand with acquiring knowledge. The methods have to be practiced, by applying them for the experience of knowledge:

- By practicing the methods we come to an experienced knowledge
- The acquisition of knowledge is deepened by practicing the methods
- Only practicing the methods can educate and form. Knowledge alone doesn't form man into the deep inner layers of the psychical life
- Knowledge without inner confrontation stays without effects on the person and his life.

■ Self-knowledge comes through training, practicing the methods. Each performance demands increased training (similar to for example: sport)

Diagram 1.13: The Methods of Self-education

 TECHNIQUES OF RELAXATION

 THINKING OPERATIONS

 INTROSPECTION

 ACQUIRE KNOWLEDGE

 FORMING IDENTITY

 WORK DIARY

 SELF-CONTROL

 CONTEMPLATION

 MENTAL-TRAINING

Life Techniques as Part of Life

We formulate from our experiences, tips and advice around everyday life, private and professional, always constructively aimed towards self-education:

1. Principle of small steps

- Reduce the aims into rough aims, these into fine aims, these into micro-steps
- A long way consists of many little parts; these again are made up of many little steps
- Working 1 hour per day = 365 hours a year = 48 days at 7.5 hours = 10 weeks
- Concentrating on the micro-level, without losing the main aim, is relieving
- Put each little building stone into a complex network

2. Processing information

- What you know thoroughly already, you shouldn't look at, read about or listen to 100 times
- Concentration focused on new, on unknown things; and managing the unknown
- Weighting information (in its meaning and actuality), giving priority
- Putting new information into a context (also the background of interests)
- Not only logical and rational understanding, but also tackling it with intuition

3. To dose the amount and the force/ to analyze the field of the forces

- Someone who is tired, performs little
- Overeating doesn't provide a good basis for working
- That which is too heavy shall be reduced to small pieces until it can be carried
- Plan your day the evening before, but finish the old day first
- Always leave some space for free time in your day-planning
- A daily routine, mostly equal or similar, helps with tedious work
- Recognizing forces which produce pressure from inside and from outside

4. Learning self-management

- He, who learns, can manage his life better, this is necessary for surviving
- Learning starts with a precise perception, a correct interpretation

- High aims always contain little steps of new learning processes
- Disturbances understood as a call for learning, and thus also an opportunity
- Recognize your biorhythm through a diary / time table

5. Intelligent (!) positive thinking

- Only naive people say 'from day to day everything goes better and better'
- You have to intelligently define what 'better' means
- Only an ignorant person thinks that shadows or suffering don't contain something positive
- What did I do well? What do I have to do differently in order to make it better?
- Happiness is never a durable state. Therefore: search for the 'positive' in the real life
- 'Positive' is firstly and simply life itself; so: live!

6. Performance is the start of every success

- From nothing comes nothing
- The more performance, the more substance
- Increase self-confidence consciously on the basis of the facts of your performance
- Take another train if the actual train doesn't take you anywhere
- A lot is important and urgent; a lot is banal, but nevertheless important
- A 100% satisfactory job does not exist
- Reflect on your performance critically in context with the human being and human life

7. To direct the perception

- Go to the back and look from there
- Involve biographical dimensions in self- and alien-perception
- Scrutinize what seems to be clear and obvious
- If somebody tells the truth, you will see from his moral performances
- The content of perception is not your life, so keep your distance!
- Never measure your life on momentary self- and alien-perception

8. Lateral thinking (the thinking which includes all sides)

- Take sentences apart, divide thoughts and put them together in a new way
- Change words and enrich them with other terms

- Put a question in another way and divide it into different single questions
- Change the sequence, put all thought in a new order
- Make a detour, the short cut is mostly the longer and wearisome way
- Go the distance with time and area, this way you can change the dimensions
- Widen the dimension of time and environment, then the facts become better balanced

9. Re-framing: give sense constructively

- Many uncomfortable facts become a positive function from another point of view
- Put the subject in another context, this way you may find a positive understanding
- Change a negative experience into a constructive philosophical image
- To take action can reduce worry and makes it possible to have new experiences
- 'Others also have problems'; you don't have to solve all problems
- Out of every humiliation you can become stronger; that's better than to become evil

10. Live the human being!

- It is better to make genuine love on a hayloft, than to make love with lies in a 'golden bed'
- To live without wisdom millions can do, it has always been like that
- To maintain health, yes, but: there are higher values than physical health
- Success without love and spirit has little to do with the human being
- Live with a certain distance from others and from all levels of hierarchy!

Notes and Perspectives

What purpose do the 10 life techniques have in everyday life?

Write down the central keywords from this sub-chapter:

What is the human being without practicing the essential methods of self-education?

Explain: Life techniques are important because...:

What did people learn about the methods of self-education in their parent's home, at school and in the church?

What importance do the 10 life techniques have in the communication between life partners and in the interactions in general?

How do the methods of self-education show themselves in politics and the economy?

What does advertising convey to us about life techniques?

Formulate an important question about the methods of self-education:

5.2. The Framework Conditions

The one, who wants to learn an instrument, has to decide: lessons, training and studying. So it is with everything, what we have to learn systematically. There is very little effect, if one learns a subject only occasionally, and this always when boredom arises.

Personality education has to be organized. This starts with some questions: What do I want? Where can I receive what I want? How can I put all the activity into a schedule? When do I train? What do I give priority to? Some habits can be useful. Each one has his own inclinations.

Some principles are beyond the individual: personality education needs time daily. Most people have enough time nowadays.

Writing down one's dreams early in the morning perhaps demands setting the alarm a little bit earlier. Some can practice small exercises to relax just for a few minutes during a break at work. Others can find a quarter of an hour during lunch time just for a small mental-exercise.

Each of us can find some time for ourselves after work, two or three times a week. Over the weekend there is a lot of free time for many self-education activities. This is then a way of life, a kind of living with love, spiritual intelligence and wisdom. In that way we don't waste our time with empty gossiping and passive consumption or aimless daydreaming.

Inner activity instead of external activity becomes a guideline, where external movements mean only wear and tear instead of a valuable life.

The integration of self-education into everyday life becomes interesting, when we envisage new life forms:

Relaxation and meditation integrated into the timetable of the work place; new institutions with programs for personality education for valuable leisure; family conferences and debates within relationships about the subject of personality education.

Seminars can be a regular part of the style of living, instead of spending the weekends doing nothing or driving around aimlessly only polluting the environment.

The media entertains mankind and offers information. Someone who can give quality to his life, can distinguish between quantity and quality, sits himself moderately in front of the television, consumes his 'leisure-beer' with style, will not occupy himself just to rid himself of frustrations, but be motivated with a love for life.

Culture as a style of life, and not as an article of consumption, integrates self-knowledge and Individuation. In self-education show, sensation, demonstration of power or a spiritual and emotional brainwashing aren't asked for.

A life in Individuation is genuine, creative, fresh, objective and substantial.

Are there arguments against such a kind of life?

Where is society heading, if nobody will live with these values anymore?

Reflections and Discussion

■ Self-knowledge and Individuation can't be elaborated on sufficiently only with courses. Practice of personality education is part of the life style, a way of living.

With each step in the process of Individuation we have new aspects of living.

Because by reaching a new purpose we find a new quality for our life. But always, during our whole lives, these activities are part of our everyday life.

Absolving courses about theories and methods is a work on the foundation. Training through courses means to apply, to widen, to deepen and to practice.

Beyond that every one has his own possibilities and inclinations, to integrate the knowledge and the methods into his everyday life.

■ The practical work of self-education, beyond courses, demands some frameworks, if it shall lead to success:

- The way of living shall provide time and space
- The sphere of life will tolerate and allow this work
- The attitudes to that work are a vital foundation
- The potential of the learning activities will be utilized by many sides

■ Stimulations to the practical work are:

- To write down daily your dreams; preferably immediately after waking up
- To relax systematically and shortly twice a day (10 min.)
- To empty the mind each evening with a short mental-exercise
- A rough timetable for the day with some keywords may reserve time for work
- To practice daily a short imagination exercise on any theme (15 min.)
- To regularly spend at weekends an hour reflecting on the past week
- To participate regularly in training courses
- To make notes about the experiences in training courses
- To read a book for a few hours a week about related subjects
- To meet new people for discussions, who also practice self-education
- To try to do new things and then to evaluate the result
- To summarize the work done and the results every few months
- To tackle in regular rotation each week an other subsystem and theme
- But: continuously working is not always possible
- Modules-courses, every 3-4 months, can always be an option

Diagram 1.14: Organization of Self-education

 Well planning of time

Positive attitudes

 Clear day purposes

 Meditation music

Right tempo

 Learning activities

 Training

Work planning

 Consider noise in the environment

 Participate on courses

Considering the environment

 Staying on the ground

 Work diary

Evaluation

Life Today as a Framework for Life Tomorrow

Some extrapolations:

- You think love isn't so important? Others think the same. All think the same. What next?
- Professors don't want wisdom; teachers don't want wisdom; students neither. Consequences?
- Some think self-knowledge is nonsense; others too; finally all think that. And now?
- Some say, only money is important; others say the same. Finally all say that. What then?
- One says: you have to be faster than others; everybody says that. What does that look like?
- First, one wins with a lie; then several; then many; then everyone. What remains?
- Many people go so far as to say 'feelings are not important'. What comes after that?
- Weak and ill people are ostracized. Imagine: from 58-85 you are weak and ill. Painful?
- Men haven't got any psychical needs; women neither. What would this look like?
- In 30 years 10 times more nuclear waste has to be administrated for 10,000 years? Costs?
- All Europeans are 50% healthier, drive 50% less. The consequences?
- All households and enterprises consume 50% less electricity. Why? How?
- 50% of Europeans pursue 1 hour of self-knowledge every day. Consequences?
- Second question during an interview for a 'top-job': How well do you know yourself?
- A teacher who has cleaned up his biography? How is the school then?
- Every European reduces 50% of his waste. What kind of consequences would that have?
- The European politicians don't lie and don't distort anymore? What happens through that?
- Priests of all religions are 'Individuated men'. What then?
- Statesmen and ministers are 'Individuated men'. How would politics be then?
- 50% of all adults in Europe reflect on their leisure life. What changes?
- Nobody is a fan of high-performance sport, but still of sport. What effects does that have?

- 10 million people demonstrate because nobody takes love seriously anymore. Imaginable?
- 1 hour of self-knowledge daily in the work place. Would every one take such a job?
- Nobody wants to learn anymore after school and professional school. Consequences?
- Life-lies stink like sewage. How would people treat each other?
- All adults read 12 books each year about the psychical life. What could change?
- The newspapers report daily about dreams from readers. Exciting reading?
- Everywhere centers for self-education. Everybody goes there. Relations in the neighborhood?
- Anyone can get married only if he has thoroughly practiced self-knowledge. Advantages?
- To beget children is forbidden without a thorough self-education. Who protests?
- Only those that strengthen their character with self-education can become managers. Bad luck?
- 75% of adults practice psycho-hygiene daily 2x10 min. How would this influence society?
- Earnings are linked to the status of the personal Individuation. Why not?
- Everybody writes on his door, what makes him happy. How would people communicate?

→ Behind the walls of indifference danger spreads.
→ Denying and 'not-seeing' the global risks represent in itself a risk.
→ Denied risks prosper especially well and very quickly.

Every individual can do a lot for himself. Nobody forces people, to perceive life risks. But the arrived risks force the human being to carry the consequences, regardless of how tragic one then suffers.

Way of Living – Critical Self-reflection

We live in a difficult époque with challenges we never had before: consumption, prosperity, comfort and an immense variety of experiences.

The external pressure is huge: already small stimuli activate sexual lust, romantic fantasy, aggressive feelings, drive to eat and to drink, etc. One doesn't know any more what is good and bad, right and wrong, true and false.

Some critical contemplation about one's own way of living includes:

- Do I feel good about my body? Can I admit body experiences?
- What do I think and feel about housework; and how do I go about it?
- Am I aware of how I dress myself and how I buy clothes?
- What are the purposes and how do I create (decorate) my living area?
- How do I care for my body? What is my attitude toward my personal hygiene?
- How do I handle the media? How do I behave in front of the TV?
- How have I furnished my bedroom? How do I feel in my bedroom?
- How do I handle food? How do I choose what I eat?
- What do I do to indulge myself? Can I enjoy and create lust?
- How do I deal with other people?
- What has high importance for me in my very personal daily life?
- Which values do I live with concentration, well aimed and decisively?
- How do I confine myself against others? (e.g. visits)
- How do I become stimulated with new ideas for my life?

Way of living – Concrete suggestions:

- Specifically looking for and taking note of positive images.
- Constructive thoughts in daily life, even with small things.
- Calming thoughts; daily 2-3 times; practicing mental fitness.
- Meditate with releasing and deliberating images.
- Creating mental distance, especially if thoughts are too cramped.
- Dissolving opposites with active meditation (visualization).
- Getting rid of inner suffering through elaboration.
- Becoming free of conflicts clarifying them, and with the right attitude.
- Accepting life positively; taking this attitude serious, even with unimportant things.
- Living needs with a clear mind; that means: balanced and at the right moment.
- Controlling perception; not wandering around with the eyes to much.
- Reducing stimuli; not focusing and empathizing too much.
- In some moments becoming free from space and time through meditation.
- Thoughtful life rhythm, also in professional moments of hectic existence.
- A healthy and holistic way of living, psychologically and physically.
- A balanced rational and intuitive understanding of one's own existence.
- Dealing with life in a combination of analytical and artistic and creative way.
- Thinking in an integrated combination of logic and spirituality.
- A networked dealing with language and images in life issues.

- Elaborating in line and synthetically at the same time. (Networked thinking).
- Taking into account the personal biorhythm especially for specific work.
- Continuously holding a certain distance to others and life themes.
- Containing topics of conversations, guiding the communication with the participants.
- Not producing too much pressure; considering the reality of meanings.
- Living in a permanent development and learning.
- Holding discipline: emotional, social, mental, moral, etc.

Notes and Perspectives

What purpose does a consciously organized self-education serve in daily life?

Write down the central keywords from this sub-chapter:

What is a human being who doesn't care about the risks (the 'eight deadly sins')?

Explain: People must organize their self-education because…:

What did people learn about the external framework for an educated human being in their parent's home, at school and in the church?

What importance does the organization of self-education have in the communication between life partners and in the interactions in general?

How do politics and the economy react to the 'eight deadly-sins'?

What does advertising convey to us about the effects from our consumption lifestyle today in 10, 20 or 30 years?

Formulate an important question about the organization of self-knowledge:

5.3. The Responsibility

No one can take away somebody else's education. Nobody can be carried along on somebody else's Individuation journey.

If no one on this earth lives love anymore, then love will die.

If nobody takes responsibility for human values, then human values will disappear from the face of the Earth.

If man doesn't make place for children and elderly people, for invalids and sick people, for weak people and indigenous populations, then humanity will disappear.

If nobody asks about the psychical life anymore, then this will manifest itself in total force by itself.

If love and spirit disappear, then hatred and chaos dominate.

History is the sum of the history of individuals in their interaction. Consequently each of us contributes our part to the evolution or to the regression, to love or to hate.

At the end of one's life each of us has to be confronted with what one has accomplished.

The question comes to each of us from inside: Have you wasted your life? What did you contribute with your life to the history of mankind?

The greatest fortune at the end of life is for everyone, if he can look back and know:

"I have gotten to know myself and educated myself, I have lived with love and spirit. More and more I became a vivid representation of the circle-cross-archetype. I gave myself from my inner life a genuine expression through Individuation. I learnt to love the values of the psychical life and I lived them in my relationships. I connected my intelligence with spirit, I lived my heart with spirit, and I bounded back my actions in the force of the spirit..."

There are certainly many people, who have no possibilities, beyond their small conditions of existence, to take responsibility for their life. Nobody can just break out from their framework of life. Some have a great possibility, and others can't find the starting point.

But anybody who has the minimal conditions, to take on to his self-education, to learn and to bring the process into a movement, stands in front of the decision, to take responsibility.

That is the essence of the question about the meaning of our existence:

Our own psychical-spiritual life is the basic theme of the human being: as a reality and as a question, as a result and as knowledge. Man owes personality education and Individuation to himself. He owes to himself, to grow and to live what he is as psychical-spiritual wholeness.

This is the responsibility that each of us has from inside, for himself and for others.

Reflections and Discussion

■ Man produces a lot of his life conditions himself. Many are changeable by himself. That means: many facts in life and their effects are variable. The affected people have a certain amount of freedom of responsibility for their actions.

■ However man lives, it has consequences for him and for others, for the environment and therein again for the human being.

We can act wrongly, do nothing or act too little. Nobody can live without this having consequences for the future.

For that reason life always exerts responsibility. Certainly there is a way out:

- Others are culpable
- Others will do it
- I will do it, when I have time...
- It is the will of God
- I feel good today, why should I worry about tomorrow?

■ Several starting points and factors occur in life, which are not caused by us, nor can they be blamed on others.

- Life is never predictable.
- Misfortune and suffering are not bad per se; often they can't be blamed on anyone.
- Misfortune and suffering are part of life.

■ A great part of the population is struck by 'destiny':

- Many are sick or suffering in their inner life
- Many are socially underprivileged and suffer from privation
- Many are put 'off-side' from the professional world through retirement
- Many are sorted out from the fight, because they are weak
- Society isn't made for children; many children are suffering because of that
- Many elderly people suffer from their ailment and loneliness
- Many people suffer from the violence caused by other people

■ What men do today for themselves they do for their future and for the future of others.

Everything that they do out of balance from their psychical life and Individuation will come back and haunt them; rejected love and the unconsidered inner Spirit can never be lost. As a reversal we all are touched.

Therefore each of us has a responsibility for himself and for the community as well.

Diagram 1.15: Sphere of Activities

Caring for the body

Psychical basic feeling

Knowledge and wisdom

Methods and their application

The holistic psychical life

One's own actions

Planning one's own life

One's own living area

Caring for animals

The life partner

One's own children

The world of children

The world of elderly people

Friends and acquantainces

The humanity

The values of life

The institutions

Cultural assets

Responsibility and Conscience

Responsibility encompasses various self-reflective questions towards one's own life culture such as: How do I eat? How do I move around with and without a car? How do I talk (on the telephone and everywhere)? How do I choose my clothes and shoes? How do I experience my living environment? How do I shape love and sexual lust? How do I do my house work? How do I deal with money? How do I choose and shape being together with other people? How do I deal with my waste? How do I deal with information? How seriously do I take my bodily needs? What do I do with my dreams? Do I take my psychical life seriously? Do I form my inner psychical being?

Responsibility is the ability and the readiness to give serious answers to an existential being addressed as a person. Being responsible is a basic state that has mandatory and unavoidable character. The absoluteness of a genuine responsibility refers to the conscience, within which the human being becomes conscious of his reasoned being.

In Individuation responsibility is bound to the inner Spirit. The question remains, what has been formed in the conscience through upbringing, education, socialization, and enculturation (assimilation of culture); In other words: what is originally genuine (therefore independent from every upbringing, from every 'Milieu').

Do we need a conscience? Without a conscience there remains only the instinctive life, or a poor instinctive life. Where does it lead us to, if nobody takes any responsibility for his life anymore? How can we take responsibility for our life, but reject self-knowledge and self-education? If man wants to communicate and decide about moral knowledge, about education of the conscience and the responsibility, he can do it as an indoctrinated existence or as a human being, well educated (trained) in self-knowledge, so that he knows well through his own experience, what the psychical life contains and also what this means for the human being.

Taking responsibility starts with changing attitudes:

- To think too much only creates problems. The future is unimportant today.
- To contemplate about one's own way of living is unimportant.
- With positive thinking one can resolve nearly all problems.
- The church teaches the path. The entire life is in the hands of God.
- The political party solves the problems of mankind.
- Sex is for people that need it. Everything producing pleasure is allowed.

- The politicians have got all problems under control.
- Work and performance have highest priority.
- Only the objective reason is important. Feelings hinder life.
- Life is like it is. To live as it arises in the moment is right.
- The past is passed. Why should I think about the past?
- Being fully stressed is quite healthy. It's good to accelerate sometimes.
- Scientific research produces progress.
- To wallow in vice is allowed as long as it doesn't disturb others.
- If you are ill, you were just unlucky.
- The law is the salvation of the people.
- Psychology is for weak people. Dreams are unimportant.
- Persons with problems are simply problematic persons.
- There has always been war and there will always be war in the future.
- What people say about damages caused to the environment is exaggerated.

Network of Self-knowledge and Self-education

Methods, life techniques, framework conditions, ways of living, responsibility

1. Being human isn't possible without learning processes. Since the earliest high cultures mankind has been reflecting, been formed and forms himself. This is partly historically conditioned and partly from the simple fact, that the human being essentially means the psychical organism.

2. However we understand the psychical forces, in importance and priority; we are forming these in the framework of our cultural environment. Every one, no matter which race, which nationality, which language or which religion has a psychical organism. Every one is only a human being through that, and he grows by forming his psychical forces to what being human potentially contains as an evolutionary process.

3. How can we guide and educate the human being without extensively knowing the psychical organism? How can we understand each other, if we understand little or nothing about the psychical reality?

4. Human development is more than accumulation of many learning processes, more than fulfillment of culturally given life plans (e.g. create a family), and more than a materialistic view we can seize. Without self-knowledge and self-education the human being has no chance to find an autonomous and rational freedom.

5. Why should we promote people in our community, who haven't got any interest in self-knowledge and self-education (but who are capable of elaborating these)? They harm the human being and its evolution.

6. Say to all people, that love doesn't have to be promoted, also the spiritual force, the truthfulness, the humility, and what the main archetype as wholeness represents... until all men on this Earth say the same: 'This isn't important...' What do we have then?

7. Imagine: Nobody on this Earth is engaged anymore to reduce hatred, greed, envy, violence, life lies, egoism, materialism, experiential addictions, desire for power and the rejection of the psychical-spiritual life. Would you like to live your old age during 20-30 years in such a world? And your children should they live in such a world?

8. Isn't it normal and obvious that if you would promote those in their activities who are of benefit for the human community, through self-education, through taking responsibility in this goal for others? Who could bring himself into play for the basic values of the human being, if he (and the values) wouldn't be promoted by society?

9. If you have investigated yourself assiduously and systematically, if you know yourself thoroughly, and if you have formed well-balanced psychical forces, wouldn't it be normal, that what you are inside and what you have formed inside, you want to live also outside?

The ability to take responsibility and to live is related with:

- Perception, Language, thinking, judging and taking conclusions
- Being aware and taking the psychical basic needs seriously
- Living the power of love: to protect, to promote, to develop, etc.
- Communicating with the inner Spirit (through dreams)
- Self-control and self-management
- Social competences and life techniques
- Taking feelings (emotions) under self-control
- A balanced unconscious

Notes and Perspectives

What purpose does responsibility and conscience serve in daily life?

Write down the central keywords from this sub-chapter:

What is the human being without responsibility for his psychical-spiritual development?

Explain: People must take on responsibility for the evolutionary human being, because...:

What did people learn about responsibility for self-education in their parent's home, at school and in the church?

What importance does responsibility for self-education have in the communication between life partners and in the interactions in general?

How do politics and the economy promote the responsibility for self-education?

What does advertising convey to us about the co-responsibility for self-education?

Formulate an important question about responsibility and conscience:

5.4. Exercises

1. Which methods of self-education do people practice?

2. Which life conditions are beneficial to people's personality education?

3. Which life conditions are hindering people's personality education?

4. Which psychical forces do people have analyzed and formed purposefully?

5. Which psychical forces do people experience as most important to form?

6. What would people's daily life be like if they integrate their personality education?

7. Life organization. Mark what applies to a majority of people:

4 = regularly
3 = often
2 = sometimes
1 = a bit/rarely
0 = never/no

☐ When I have a problem, I deal with it systematically.
☐ I think about, what is the right moment to tackle pending difficulties.
☐ When I retire myself to reflect, I reduce noisy and disturbing factors.
☐ I use methods to relax myself.
☐ I apply a technique to clear my thoughts.
☐ When I am occupied with memories, I try to understand them.
☐ I keep a diary/dream diary/working diary.
☐ I have my "tricks", how to deal with myself when I am in a bad mood.
☐ I know what time of the day I am disposed for defined specific work.
☐ I interpret my dreams.
☐ I meditate according to clear rules and working steps.
☐ I regulate closeness and distance to the facts of everyday life.
☐ I have meditation music at home and I use it.
☐ I formulate my inner difficulties and emotions.
☐ I have a place in my home, where I can write and study.
☐ I regularly buy books to widen my mind.
☐ I have good self-control when I am talking on the telephone.
☐ I consciously control myself during conversations with others.
☐ When I am preoccupied with something, I deal with it systematically.
☐ I can accept, when I have difficulties with myself.
☐ I take my time to gain an overview over the way I create my life.
☐ I keep a list about the small things I have to do.
☐ I meditate about archetypal symbols.
☐ I take care of my self-identity and I widen it as a man/woman.
☐ I consciously take time to be alone.
☐ My physical (body) self-experience is important for me.
☐ I look for variety in my leisure.
☐ I have a good overview about what my life contains.

Total points: …..

What do you conclude from this result?

8. Difficulties with life techniques

Put into words what seems difficult for people from the following 10 life techniques:

• Principle of the small steps:	
• Elaborating information:	
• Dose the quantity and the forces:	
• Self-management with learning:	
• Intelligent positive thinking:	
• Performance for success:	
• Directing perception:	
• Lateral thinking:	
• Re-Framing. Constructive sense:	
• To live the human being:	

9. Competences of methods. Note some important questions and statements about the following methods:

• Techniques of relaxation:	
• Operation of thinking:	
• Introspection:	
• Acquiring knowledge:	
• Forming the self-identity:	
• Keep a diary:	
• Self-control:	
• Contemplation:	
• Mental-Training:	

How do you value your knowledge and skills of those methods?

Multiple Choice Test

Choose the four correct answers and mark them with a cross: ☒ a) lust

5.1. The practical methods: The important practical methods of the personality education and Individuation are:

☐ a) Autogenous training
☐ b) Practical imagination
☐ c) Dream interpretation
☐ d) Healthy   cooking
☐ e) Producing enlightenment
☐ f) Contemplation

5.2. The framework conditions: Elemental framework conditions of personality education are:

☐ a) Helpful friends
☐ b) To write down dreams everyday
☐ c) Acquiring a lot of knowledge
☐ d) To meditate regularly
☐ e) To live as a vegetarian
☐ f) To keep a working diary

5.3. The responsibility: The following statements are a consequence of personality education to the aspect of responsibility:

☐ a) We can change many social problems with self-education.
☐ b) Every one has a responsibility for the values, which he is living.
☐ c) What everyone lives, has an effect on him and on the collective.
☐ d) The considerations of the psychical life are always exaggerated.
☐ e) Man has a responsibility towards himself and others for everything,
     that he doesn't do, but could do about self-education.
☐ f) Responsibility towards Individuation relates only to a personal
     interest in life.

6. Self-management in Everyday Life

He, who understands how to guide himself in a balanced way and taking into consideration the network of the environment, has the best chances of a happy and successful life.

Essential Theses

❑ To self-management in the individual life sphere belongs the question: "What do I use my time for?"

❑ A conscious and planned time organization is as important in private life as in the professional world.

❑ In all sectors of the private life it is valuable and beneficial, to regularly make order; these are for example:

- Individual administration
- Clothes
- Wishes for leisure
- Relationships
- Loft, cellar, cupboard
- Acquaintances
- further education
- Wishes for consumption

❑ Also in the personal life (and not only in the working world) it is important to apply detailed planning to your own goals.

❑ Creativity is essential for a satisfactory creation of life. Individual problems can be solved more efficiently with creativity. A 'good' relationship lives considerably from creativity of both partners.

❑ Creativity is useful in many life areas and allows:

- To make more of oneself
- To make habits flexible
- To live with lust and joy
- To live new situations in a new way
- To widen norms and values
- To practice self-education

❑ Creativity can be promoted multilaterally, for example with:
- Imagination
- Inspiration
- Keeping a diary
- Loving
- Elaborating experiences
- To value intuition

6.1. Self-management and Time Organization

'To manage' means: to lead, create, skillfully contrive, organize and guide; terms which are used in the business world, in a factory and enterprise; and here: for the individual life.

It is said 'time is money'. The main question during the last hours of a person's life is certainly: 'What have you done with your life (your time and your possibilities)?' Many people waste their time and don't look after their real possibilities enough.

Many have the 'post-modern philosophy': to enjoy, relax, experience an exciting life, be lazy, earn money, not take life too seriously, gossip, live like Casanova, just stay cool, etc. Why couldn't self-management be an alternative?

Life time can be divided into 4 phases:

1) Childhood/youth: until approximately the age of 20.
2) Approximately 10 years to build up a professional and personal life.
3) Approximately 35-40 years of professional life.
4) 15-30 years in retirement.

The working time is approximately 35 hours a week (or less; and many are unemployed for a long period). Thus, a lot of time is left for the personal life.

These are enormous opportunities for personal interests: self-realization in the true sense of the word; commitments to ideas and humanistic values (culture, society, politics etc.); genuine self-fulfillment!

Neither a career nor an academic education is needed to perform a 'great project' in life.

Yet most people see time disappear: 15-20 hours of watching TV per week; 10 hours and more chatting about content without individual interest; more than 10 hours hanging around, plus the varied time-consumers like phone calls, reading newspapers, visits, little quarrels in relationships without results, waiting in a traffic jam, lack of personal organization, etc. All this summed up over the years of a life. Years of lifetime lost! And then the 'doing nothing' in old age! Self-management is unavoidable for self-fulfillment.

A lot of time also gets lost because of psychical forces which slow down daily activities, for example a heavy biography; or needs which are not integrated; or lack of thinking; or lack of accurate behavior; or lack of a capacity of love.

He who dreams a lot, but is unable to handle his dreams constructively, loses time. Ties to ideals, values and beliefs which are to be revised imply a loss of time. Thus they are a waste of life.

A habit of defense mechanism blocks the daily course of life. He who doesn't take his body seriously as a potential for life, creates problems.

The body needs movement, a correct nutrition, agreeable clothing, lust satisfaction, experiencing nature, a balance between tension and relaxation, care for senses, simply: a positive care for the 'ego'.

Human beings stand in a complex networked environment. Also here one must consider many factors, if one wants to constructively realize one's own aims of life.

→ A conscious self-management and a thought through time organization is valuable.

Reflections and discussion

■ A basic question about consciously guided time organization is: 'What do I use my free time for?' Some examples:

Driving to work	Reading newspapers	Toilet	Getting dressed
House work	Chatting	Talking on the phone	Curiosity for events
Searching for things	Un-lust/lack of drive	Watching TV	Waiting
Impatience	Taking decisions	Traffic jams	Not listening

Haste	Unplanned shopping	No order in dossiers	Wrong planning
Visits	Paperwork	Short visits to pubs	Discussions

■ A constructive control of time usage:

Recognize time wasters	Communicate consciously	Plan the day in the morning
Start slowly	Quarrel constructively	Weekly plan
Check lists (e.g. travel)	Not always hesitating	Check through daily aims
Say 'no' (or 'yes')	Make a shopping list	Prepare telephone calls
Regulate stress	Reflected mobility	Organized documents
Recognize urgency	Take breaks as important	Define small aims for the day
Recognize importance	Overview courses of action	Concentrate during meetings

■ These are central questions for a conscious shaping of life:

- What do I want to talk about on the phone and how long do I want to talk/listen?
- Do I want to be disturbed by a phone call during a meal or when in the bathtub?
- Do I have to go shopping five times by car just for some small things?
- What do I gain by hanging around and chatting in a pub twice a week?
- Do I seriously want that? Does this have to be just now?
- What do I want to experience this year? Can I plan that ahead?
- How can I do my house work efficiently and with rational time saving?
- Should I try some new ideas? Or do I always have to imitate my parents?
- Have I created my personal living sphere?
- Do I have to know so much about other people?
- Do I constantly waste opportunities, because 'I simply don't want'?
- Do I really have no time for these new ideas or am I simply too indolent?
- What have I gained from that TV-broadcast for my life?

■ An optimal life-management includes systematically planning time for self-education.

Diagram 1.16: Control of Time Usage

CONTROL OF EFFICIENCY-UTILIZATION-TIME

To what end?	How?	Power?
	Strategy	Self-feeling
Importance	Management	Energy
Urgency	View	State of Health
Meaning	"Zoom"	Stress
Value	Will	Flexibility
Sense	Proceeding	Yes-No-Ability to Decide
Purpose	Forced by Object Facts	
Aim		

Self-management in Leisure

Positive aspects of leisure are:		Negative aspects of leisure are:	
● Joy	● Dreams	● Loneliness	● Frustration
● Experiences	● Being free	● Illusions	● Resignation
● Interests	● Sun	● Distraction	● Un-lust
● Recharging energy	● Relaxation	● Trauma	● Waste
● Revitalization	● Understanding	● Destruction	● Boredom
● Individuation	● Pleasure	● Lack of ideas	● Loneliness

The way time after work is used can make you ill:

● The same rhythm as at work continues: one stays in routine with body, mind and soul. Consequences are: rigid structures, subdivision in fixed points, inability to let things go...
● Tendency to passivity and susceptibility: just relax from the working day for the next working day...
● Tendency to ritualize: The after-work time goes more or less according to uniform schemes...to be fit for the next day...
● Alone in the community...in the family...being with others; but each one stays broadly isolated. The contacts are superficial...
● Poor 'after-work-sexuality': large discrepancy...between expectation and fantasies for erotic events and real practice...small quality of practicing
● Bad mood: ...rather negative, easily irritable. Physical and mental tiredness and feelings of failure and excessive demands play a role, caused by an unrealistic self-expectation...

Many experience boredom:

● General state of not being satisfied
● Lack of impulses and drive to do something
● Life seems to have no sense and is empty
● The person is apathetic, without strength, tired and without any willpower
● Interests and lust for life is lacking

- Time goes by slowly
- There appears to be nothing that can get rid of boredom

Stress in leisure time is caused from:

● Crowds, narrowness, queuing	● Being in boring company
● Being disturbed by others	● Always taking into account others
● Family meetings, visiting relatives	● Constant background music
● Traffic jams (waiting)	● Making too many plans
● Shopping for presents	● Boredom during weekends
● Noise pollution	● Being completely alone

Reactions are:

- Inner restlessness: nervousness, lack of concentration
- Over-sensitivity, dissatisfaction with oneself
- Feeling unwell: physical uneasiness, lack of appetite, pressure in the stomach
- Being aggressive: slamming the door, lack of order, swearing, quarrelling
- Calming down: sportive performances, going to the pub (bar), shopping...
- Distraction: withdrawing (also to bed), watching TV...

Self-management as a Call for Success

Some suggestions for your self-management:

- You need time for yourself; that means: nobody has to be reachable and accessible at every time of the day. Everybody needs his calm moments sometimes, with the mobile phone switched off. Relax every day for 5-10 minutes.
- To say 'no' without frustrating the other person, is an art. On the other hand one has to be able to say 'yes' and to account for his 'yes' and 'no'. Therefore it is recommendable to think precisely how and why one has to say 'yes' and 'no'.
- Identifying troubles gives us orientation. Strategies for problem solving make life easier. Noise and clutter produce troubles and disturbances.

Difficulties in a proceeding create disturbance. Life includes troubles and disturbances; these parts of life need to be managed.

- Thinking and acting aim-oriented; that means: plan everyday actions in the perspective of long term personal aims. To practice this, one needs to keep a journal.

- Aspire for your determined aims with a timetable and with working methods. For that, one sometimes has to read a book to get new suggestions and inspirations. Or ask others about their experiences. Never be afraid of asking for advice.

- Divide high (big) aims of life into small constructive steps. Each life phase has its own goals. And don't miss out on living the present!

- Prestige, money and success are not the highest aims of life! Reflect upon your consumption, your compensating behavior. Search for the meaning of your life inside in your soul.

- Concentrate on your energy use. Don't dissipate your forces in the chaos and in the lack of planning. One has to recharge one's energy daily. There are several techniques for relaxation.

- Ascertain priorities, which lead to determined aims. The truthful life is the essential aim of life. Also working is living. And never forget: Life lies don't lead to a good and fulfilled life.

- Not everything is equally important and urgent. Importance means: aim and success. Urgency means: time and fixed date. Urgency goes before importance. Start every week with the question: What is important for me and what is urgent this week?

- Deal with the daily matters, but also with the long term aims. Where do you want to be in 1-3 years? Check periodically if you can achieve your determined aims with your way of living.

- Regularly control your use of time. Make a day to day plan for the week, integrating your time use. Your life time is your capital; have you invested this capital well this week?

- Control your stress factors in order for them not to control you. Plan your mobility. Caution: even people, TV-news, advertisements, articles in newspapers, etc., are often stress factors.

Bear in mind:

Nobody is interested if you live a good self-management and succeed. Nobody is interested if you psychically and physically ruin yourself or if you live in a healthy way, if you have a happy relationship or if you become lonely, if you find your meaning of life or if you lead an enslaved and manipulated life such as the one represented in our zeitgeist.

Eliminate boredom and empty moments by:

- Giving yourself and your life the necessary importance
- Going ahead with your self-knowledge and work through your biography
- Taking time for your dreams (interpreting them) and meditate correctly
- Drawing your visions for your life aims and searching for the meaning of life inside
- Preparing by planning the day and the weekend in advance
- Keeping precise planning of your time also for daily odds and ends
- Keeping a diary and writing down your dreams, thoughts ideas, plans
- Strengthening your self-guidance with a well aimed personality education
- Being responsible for your own life and forming your destiny from inside

Notes and Perspectives

What purpose does an efficient time control and time usage serve in daily life?

Write down the central keywords from this sub-chapter:

What is the human being without a learned conscious self-management?

Explain: Self-management should be important to all people because...:

What did people learn about self-management in their parent's home, at school and in the church?

What importance does self-management have in the communication between life partners and in the interactions in general?

Where in politics and the economy can we see a lack of time and efficiency control?

What does advertising convey to us about self-management?

Formulate an important question about self-management:

6.2. Planning and Organization in Life

'Actually I would like to...', 'If I had time, I would...', or 'Oh, that's not possible ...': similar phrases block valuable possibilities. They undermine motivation and élan. Some would like to meet new people; others 'dream' about a cultural trip; others want to invite friends to a concert; and many more wish to learn new languages or important life knowledge. Always it's not possible 'right now'. Either there is a lack of money or time just at that moment, or something else has priority.

Chances are put into a drawer. Years pass by. In the last moment 'arguments' always become an obstacle: 'I am not able to do this now anyhow', 'That is rather unusually new', 'Anyway, I have a lot to do', and so on.

A solution could be: planning! What somebody would like to do today can be realized in a few months or in a year. That means: firstly fixing an aim, then decide on priority and finally making preparations. Instead of letting many wishes and plans in disorder on the table, the good aims and the respective preparation receive a place in the life time.

If one doesn't make plans to write down his dreams after breakfast, he will never do it regularly. If one doesn't plan the house work, it will never get done. This creates dissatisfaction. Unanswered letters become a burden with the time.

He who has to talk about important matters on the phone, but doesn't think when the right time is given, runs the risk of clearing important matters at the wrong time. This inevitably leads to failure. One can shop for clothes 'with pleasure and mood', but not be happy with his purchase. With the wrong mood we mostly reach a wrong result.

Thus: planning! Sit down, make a list of the needs, draw a timetable and make a budget, cautiously take all steps into your hands. This leads to success! Time and money can be saved, frustration and conflicts avoided. The risk of wrong actions can be reduced to a low level. The individual life receives a meaningful structure.

We can define and plan aims, what we want to do with whom: with the life partner, with children, with a friend, with parents, with colleagues, with neighbors, etc. This way everybody can take his own wishes meaningfully into his hands. That way one isn't leaving everything to 'chance'. We can take our destiny in our hands.

It doesn't matter if we have to postpone certain important wishes for months or a couple of years. It is only important, that you follow the path of your planning, without losing flexibility. Certainly, we can't always plan our life completely with thinking and with a 'mechanical' guidance.

It also may be that for high aims we have to prepare ourselves during a long time: sometimes we firstly have to reach the steps in between.

→ Thus: plan your 'one day I will...'

Reflections and Discussion

■ With planning we can reach better aims more successfully:

- Make a list of books for your further education
- Consumption needs and time can be planned within a family and in a 'single' household
- You can plan and consciously create your relationships and leisure contacts
- Leisure activities shouldn't always depend on your lust and mood
- If you want to give a deeper sense to your leisure activities, draft and plan them
- If something doesn't contribute to achieving certain aims, put it back in the right place
- You can systematically deal with your weakness to reach specific aims
- Goals and plans are only effective, when you write them down and take them seriously
- The more precisely you define your aims, the more securely they can be reached
- Some subjects can be postponed, others you should do at once
- Discuss your wishes and expectations early with the people concerned
- Revise your checklist daily and cross out the finished points with success/failure

■ It won't do any harm, if you create order in your private life, in relationships, activities and goods. A checklist for a critical view of the situation:

Casual acquaintances	A 'possible' intimate relationship
Unspoken subjects in marriage	Heaps of paper on the table and in the drawer
Needs and wishes of consumption	Ideas for further education
Wishes for weekend amusements	Hobbies (starting or neglecting)
Difficulties in relationships	Concerns of friends and acquaintances
Little vices and tics	Habits
General education (courses, reading)	Order around the living area
Attic and cellar (clearing)	Old clothes and odds and ends
Suppressing annoying subjects	To speak about wishes (not suppress them)
No folder, no place for files	No desk for studying and writing

■ Tackling and clearing of troubles in the individual life creation:

- Being addressed at the wrong time
- Lack of praise (valuation) and reinforcement
- Untidiness of others (in the family / living community)
- Lack of clear distribution of duty and responsibility (in family / living community)
- Being annoyed by music, television (noise) (in family / living community)
- Lack of transparency about what the others want (in family / living community / leisure)
- Impatience, haste, grumbling, compulsive criticizing
- Killer-phrases of others like 'that doesn't suit me now', 'we do it like that'

Diagram 1.17: From Chaos to Planning

★ Self-determined		Alien-determined	⊖
★ Order		Disorder	⊖
★ Planning		By accident	⊖
★ Structure		Chaos	⊖
★ Overview		Lack of orientation	⊖
★ Clearness		Vagueness	⊖
★ Aim-precision		Aim-diffusion	⊖
★ Decision		Indecision	⊖
★ Self-management		Self-"tatter"	⊖
★ Seriousness		Indifference	⊖
★ Well-measured speed		Haste	⊖
★ Freedom		Compulsion	⊖
★ Transparency		Non-transparency	⊖
★ Precision		Inexactitude	⊖
★ Result of thinking		Indoctrination	⊖
★ Learning		Repetition	⊖
★ Moderation		Excess	⊖

Success through Working Effectively

There are hundreds of recipes for success about how to find happiness. You can find countless books that offer the 'silver bullet' for a fast and very easy fulfillment of any desires. Some business people say anybody that doesn't want this 'silver bullet', is responsible for their own failure. There is even worse: some promise a solution of striking simplicity wrapped in hype, all this without even having to learn anything, waiting to be opened with the secret key. The slogan: You haven't got to do anything! Everything is easy and success is guaranteed. Now the fulfillment of all wishes is ready. From the moment you realize this, success is achieved in all life areas. Trust in the omnipotence of the magic words about success, and you are a good person. Subordinate yourself under the genial program of success, and you are rewarded with success. Yield to the authority, and you get the fast happy life. If you get it, you are a better person. And only such supermen can be winners. All others are losers; they are the people on the lower level; they are guilty, because they failed. Therefore: Be a millionaire! Win!

The external success is well known and socially appreciated, because it reflects the social collective neurosis: money, properties, career, reputation, power, appearance. The inner success is difficult to see, and doesn't produce more money or social recognition: fulfillment of life, self-realization, performance as an expression of talents, psychical freedom, love, security, etc. But also the inner success demands commitment of forces and resources, hard and thorough work, endurance, stamina, social competences, self-management, abilities to think and judge, ability for making compromises, understanding, etc.

The following questions concern professional activities. But all self-critical aspects have a high meaning also for the individual life. Add a specific idea to the following statements.

Success always requires strenuous work, for example:

- Do you concentrate on your thinking and the way you act?
- Are you ready to invest 'work' into your life wishes?
- Have you searched your mind for old patterns that still persist?
- Do you know that efficiency is more an art than a technique or science?
- Have you defined for yourself your aims; have you taken responsibility to reach them?
- Do you try to solve problems simply and reasonably?
- Do you distinguish between urgent and important problems?
- Have you ever made an analysis about your time usage?

- Do you have space in your time planning for unexpected events?
- Do you know what you should stop doing?
- Do you ask yourself before you start a task: "Is this the best use of time and energy?"
- Do you have a healthy self-consciousness and self-confidence?
- Do you concede the first place to your own needs?
- Do you take responsibility for your feelings?
- Can you count on your own forces, skills and character?
- Are you aware that perfectionism can hinder your effectiveness?
- Do you have courage to act and can you deal with calculated risks?
- Do you try consciously to improve your communication?
- Do you try to work together with others or against them?
- Did you take steps, to limit interruptions to the necessity?

The Basic Demand of Life: Permanent Learning

Self-management demands permanent new learning. Learning itself must follow specific rules. Effective learning doesn't just happen by itself. We summarize the central ideas of 25 learning principles:

1. Behavior of adults is changeable; learning throughout the whole life is possible.
2. Self-concept (self-identity) and self-valuation influence learning.
3. Early learning experiences promote or hinder learning.
4. Early learning experiences should be taken into consideration and respected.
5. New learning should be bound up with early learning experiences.
6. Passed experiences become more important with increasing age.
7. A positive self-concept and an optimistic self-esteem support learning processes.
8. Being endowed with learning strategies and learning abilities improves learning.
9. Changes in values, attitudes, abilities etc. destabilize at the beginning.
10. Needs and feelings influence learning processes.
11. Referring to actual developments, life crises etc. activates motivation.
12. Learning is always connected with expectations, value systems and life style of the learning person.
13. Needs of learning and alternatives must be taken into consideration.
14. Self-chosen directions of development support the learning progress.
15. Voluntary decision to learn reduces anxiety and feelings of threat.
16. Feedback is a basic precondition for learning success.
17. Learning success motivates.

18. Stress reactions through learning activities have to be taken into consideration.
19. Stress through learning isn't the same as 'learning difficulties'.
20. Keeping the learning pace flexible; because rigid time organization inhibits learning.
21. Learning without referring to life is experienced as 'lost time'.
22. Being healthy and rested are basic conditions for successful learning.
23. Use listening and seeing for learning, and don't hamper it.
24. Each adult has his individual style of learning.
25. Learning activities should be organized in sequences, cycles and have to be purposeful.

Our thesis: Steady new learning in all areas of life is a basic pre-condition for personality education and psychical-spiritual development. A person, who doesn't regularly learn anew, loses himself, wastes his potential and his self-realization.

Learning throughout the entire life - forming oneself for the whole life:

Many social areas change and widen year by year. Human beings are challenged with their whole psychical organism, with their body and with their activities. Human beings are no more confronted with nature (from that they don't know much). Some keywords to this are:

● Chemicals in the nature	● Cosmetic products
● Chemicals in food	● Multicultural society
● Payment systems	● Unemployment
● Insurance business	● Energy consumption and its effects
● Art and culture	● Cultivation
● Medicine, medical herbs, tranquillizers	● Poison
● Consumer protection (rights)	● Detergents
● Dealing with waste (rubbish) of all kind	● Excise items (its dangers)
● Clothes (synthetic material)	● Media and information

Notes and Perspectives

What purpose does planning and organizing serve in daily life?

Write down the central keywords from this sub-chapter:

What is the human being without life long and broad learning?

Explain: Working effectively is important because…:

What did people learn about 'planning instead of chaos' in their parent's home, at school and in the church?

What importance does life long (and broad) learning have in the communication between life partners and in the interactions in general?

How do politics and the economy promote life long and broad learning?

What does advertising convey to us about "planning instead of chaos"?

Formulate an important question about life long learning:

6.3. Creative Shaping of Life

Human beings are neither 'machines' nor products, nor 'an accident'. Everybody has within himself a potential of creative forces which allows him to guide his life with planning and at the same time with creativity, beyond his learned patterns. There are limits, for example individual manifold ideas or thinking potential or vitality and external possibilities.

Creativity means force to create. The psychical energy drive, the uncommon associating and the transfer of learned issues to something new are the performing forces of a creative human being. We know creativity of artists, architects and publicity managers. Making music, painting, doing handicrafts and hobbies are also creative activities. But also in everyday life creative forces play an important role.

To name but a few examples: cooking, setting the table, playing, decorating the apartment, amorous play, dancing. Communication can also be creative with intonation, choosing words, illustrations, combinations of subjects, mimic and gestures.

By using and forming symbols we are creative. Creativity can contain a purpose, but is firstly an original expression of a way of life, a style of life. With that we impart values and meaning, attract or reject others, generate stimuli and effects. A creative person creates new things in his life.

We can also treat and solve problems with creativity. Intuition, inspiration and imagination (also fantasy) are a source of this creative force. Being creative means to restructure knowledge and experiences; it also means to discover new relations between elements with spontaneity and flexibility. This includes interpretation and understanding.

Dealing with subjects of everyday life demands an active critical confrontation with oneself, with others and with the environment.

An unprejudiced perception of problems and a free way of dealing with problems are preconditions for creative problem solving. The quality of each solution depends considerably on information, however common the problem may be. To collect information is a creative activity.

We can play through (trial) each variation of a solution with sufficient information. This way, we can widen the narrow limitations of the previously given information.

The 'sudden idea' (aha-experiences, the 'I've got it') doesn't come by accident, but thoroughly thought through and creatively prepared enlightenment. New learning processes, embedded in the elaboration and evaluation of new solutions automatically follow.

Creative forming also demands questions such as:

- Can I apply it?
- Can I use it?
- Can I carry it through?
- How does it work?
- What is the 'price' of the effort?
- How can I discuss this with the people involved?

Thinking processes, memory, valuation and behavior contribute to it. Creativity determines and promotes (in everyday life): psychical health, ego-strength, delight in discovering, energy potentials, tolerance for frustration and conflicts, acceptance of complexity of everything, open mindedness and courage for autonomy for an individual life style.

Reflections and Discussion

■ Creativity is a way of shaping life, for example:

▪ Creating living area	▪ Creating tone	▪ Creating movements
▪ Creating communication	▪ Creating solutions	▪ Technical creation

■ Creativity means:

- Ability to make more of oneself
- To create new ideas, to change old images through new ones
- To replace habit-patterns through new and more suitable ones
- To think of something and to realize it, what others haven't discovered yet
- To deal flexibly, spontaneously and open-mindedly with new situations
- To see situations (problems, conflicts) in new perspectives
- To broaden the individual limits of norms and values

- To practice lust of living and creating as a form of active life
- Putting new information together, to combine in a new way for the individual

■ Creative forces can be improved through:

• Meditation	• Imagination	• Daydreaming
• Keeping a diary	• Developing self-confidence	• Loving and living
• Reading	• Elaborating experiences	• Living spirituality
• Accepting anxiety (fear)	• Taking the inner voice seriously	• Notes and drafts
• Training body language	• Brainstorming/mind-mapping	• Active confrontation

■ Conditions for creativity are:

• Group influences	• Kind of situation	• Solution of a situation
• Self-evaluation	• Communication	• Vitality
• Joy of life	• Autonomy	• Relief of trouble factors

■ The following characteristics of personality promote creative forces:

• Ability to think	• Health	• Emotional security
• Ability to imagine	• Freshness and being awake	• Lust on forms
• Enjoying daydreaming	• Sensitivity	• Interest to discover
• Drive	• Ability to judge	• Joy to create
• Independency	• Memory performance	• Ability to associate
• Courage	• Openness to dreams	• Acceptance of stress

Diagram 1.18: Potentials of Creativity

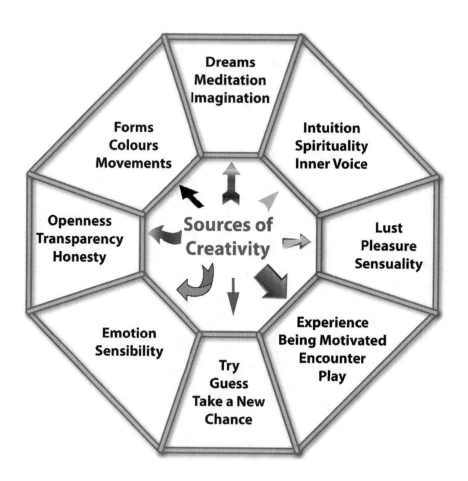

Dreams
Meditation
Imagination

Forms
Colours
Movements

Intuition
Spirituality
Inner Voice

Openness
Transparency
Honesty

Sources of Creativity

Lust
Pleasure
Sensuality

Emotion
Sensibility

Try
Guess
Take a New
Chance

Experience
Being Motivated
Encounter
Play

Creative Techniques for Resolving Problems

Creativity is decisive in the elaboration of problems. But creativity is not simply an accidental product that emerges from the chaos of an inner emotional state.

Creativity needs the management from the person (the 'ego'). Creativity is a richness of ideas from an inner source.

Creativity is a holistic experience and elaboration, more imaginative than rational (intellectual). But to actively use creativity, one needs techniques that have to be learnt as to how to handle it.

Some suggestions, how you can effectively tackle problems:

- Take the time to understand the problem before you start solving it
- Keep all facts clear in your mind
- Identify the facts which are especially important
- Prepare a list of questions to deal with the problem
- Try to be consciously original and to find new ideas
- It isn't ridiculous if you say anything uncommon or if you are wrong
- Rid yourself of cultural taboos which could undermine a possible solutions
- Draw a diagram to visualize the problem
- Write down your ideas to retain important facts and to find models
- Imagine how you will solve the problem
- Go through the real elements of the problem
- Divide the problem into parts: solve a part and continue like that
- Use analogies (similar situations), examine the possibility for transfer
- Keep your mind open, if an attempt doesn't work, examine the presumption
- Use different strategies: verbal, visual, calculating, action
- If you are stuck in an attempt, try another way to go ahead for the solution
- Be watchful of strange or plotting situations. You could be near a solution
- Search for connections between different facts
- Trust your intuition. Approach a way and look where it leads to
- Try to guess the way for a solution, more and more until it goes ahead
- Think about an uncommon manner to use things and the environment
- To make a great fuss may slow down, but can finally lead to the goal
- Jump over common things, try to invent new methods
- Try to be objective; evaluate your ideas as if they were alien
- Activate your delight of discovering through variable interpretations

- Limit norms and 'zeitgeist', which over all support the pressure for 'belonging'
- Search uncommon places for more information about the facts
- Daydream a 'successful story' about the problem
- Ask your dreams about explanations and solutions
- Widen the problem with new elements, you can perhaps live with
- Enlarge or decrease elements, this helps to find solutions
- Strengthen the weakest parts of a solving strategy and of an effort
- Search complementary parts and thus widen the picture of the problem

Performance, Concentration, Memory

The physical readiness of performance

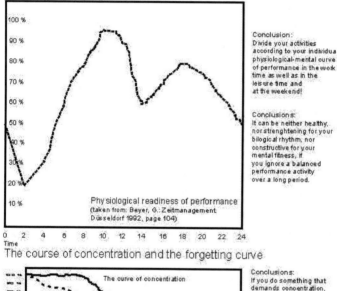

Conclusion:
Divide your activities according to your individual physiological-mental curve of performance in the work time as well as in the leisure time and at the weekend!

Conclusions:
It can be neither healthy, nor strenghtening for your bilogical rhythm, nor constructive for your mental fitness, if you ignore a balanced performance activity over a long period.

Physiological readiness of performance
(taken from: Beyer, G.: Zeitmanagement Düsseldorf 1992, page 104)

The course of concentration and the forgetting curve

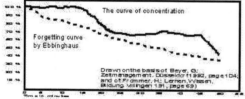

The curve of concentration

Forgetting curve by Ebbinghaus

Drawn on the basis of Beyer, G.: Zeitmanagement. Düsseldorf 1992, page 104; and of Frommer, H.: Lernen, Wissen, Bildung Villingen 1931, page 69)

Conclusions:
If you do something that demands concentration, take a brake regulary after each 45 minutes.

Conclusions:
Learn always with repetition! This is the way that it remains in the memory!

Professor Hans Aebli refers to results of investigation, which have also a decisive significance in the daily life:
"... Meaningful and understood material are less forgotten than meaningless and misunderstud (material) ...
Distributed repetitions create faster progress of learning than (just) added..."
(From: Zwölf Grundformen des Lehrens. Stuttgart 1983, page 339)

Notes and Perspectives

What purpose does creativity serve in the personal daily life?

Write down the central keywords from this sub-chapter:

What is the human being without the use of the potentials of creativity?

Explain: Creativity is important for people's life because…:

What did people learn about the potential of creativity in their parent's home, at school and in the church?

What importance does creativity with all its aspects have in the communication between life partners and in the interactions in general?

Where can we see a lack of creative problem solving in politics and the economy?

What does advertising convey to us about a creative lifestyle?

Formulate an important question about creativity:

6.4. Exercises

1. What are the people's attitudes about the self-management?

2. In which personal life areas aren't people controlling their use of time enough?

3. Which forces of creativity trouble people mostly?

4. Why do people ignore a creative and an efficient self- and time-management?

5. What is the real benefit from a successful creative activity for problem solving?

6. Why are a majority of people not creative in resolving their problems?

7. Use of time. Note the daily use of time in minutes (weekly average):

... Going to work
... Reading books
... Toilette
... Getting dressed
... House work
... Chatting
... Phoning
... Curiosity on events
... Searching for things
... Lack of drive
... Watching TV
... Waiting
... Restless
... Finding decisions
... Traffic jams/lights
... Not listening clearly
... Haste
... Buying without plan
... Paperwork
... Searching for something
... Visits
... Visiting pubs
... False planning
... Discussions
... Eating
... Cooking
... Dish-washing
... Playing
... Reading the paper
... Professional reading
... Further education
... Hanging around
... Listening to music
... Hobbies
... Decorating rooms
... Buying small things
... Health
... Reinforcement
... Collecting info
... Doing for others
... Dream interpretation

... Keeping a diary
... Meditation
... Adventures
... Body experience
... Preoccupation
... Relaxation
... Love and relationship

Your conclusions:

8. Success through working and living effectively. Respond with a short sentence:

- How do people concentrate on the results of their doing?
- How do people invest time and work for their wishes?
- How do people investigate their thinking and judging (evaluating)?
- Which own small but essential aims have people determined for themselves?
- How do people try to objectively and reasonably solve problems?
- Are people distinguishing between urgent and important problems?
- Have people calculated their need of time for a determined concern?
- Does people's time planning give some space for unexpected things/facts/events?
- In important situations what should people generally refrain from doing?
- How do people clarify if their time and forces are used optimally?
- Which priority of values do people give their inner needs?
- How do people take responsibility for their emotions?
- How do people care for their forces and weakness?
- Where do people have courage to act and try something new with calculated risk?

9. Learning and working: Write down some stimulating keywords to each point:

- The professional and personal behavior is changeable.
- The self-identity and the self-valuation influence working and learning.
- Earlier learning experiences support or hinder the new learning and working.
- Relating earlier learning experiences with the new learning and working.

- A positive self-concept and an optimistic self-assessment promote working.
- Disposing of learning strategies and learning abilities optimizes the learning processes.
- Changes in values, attitudes, abilities, etc. destabilize at first.
- One's own needs and emotions influence the learning and working.
- A working process is influenced by expectations, values and life style of the working person.
- Self-selected development perspectives support the progress of learning.
- Success in learning motivates for working.
- Stress from learning is not the same as difficulties of learning and working.
- Being flexible in using time; too strict timings hinder and block.
- Being healthy and relaxed are basic conditions for successful working.
- Watching and listening with concentrated application.

Multiple Choice Test

Choose the four correct answers and mark them with a cross: ☒ a) lust

6.1. Which are the central activities to control time-usage?

☐ a) Always wash the dishes immediately
☐ b) Short coffee-breaks
☐ c) To plan mobility
☐ d) To overview the activities
☐ e) To recognize importance
☐ f) Check through the weekly aims

6.2. Planning and order in the personal life means:

☐ a) To always control thoughts and fantasies.
☐ b) To make a list about the books for individual education (to inform yourself).
☐ c) To discuss wishes and expectations with the people concerned.
☐ d) To write down (brainstorming), to make plans and to draw diagrams.
☐ e) To organize the needs of consumption in a daily, weekly and annual plan.
☐ f) To interpret the troubling factors under new aspects.

6.3. The following characteristics of personality increase creativity, if they are formed consciously:

☐ a) Openness for dreams
☐ b) Stress
☐ c) Openness for experience
☐ d) Ability for imagination
☐ e) Eating and drinking
☐ f) Lust to discover

7. Biographical Reflection

The human being is essentially a 'product' of his biography and how he educates and transforms himself with a critical self-reflection.

Essential Theses

❑ Everybody has his individual unmistakable history of life with the following essential 'ramification' (beside others):

- School
- Style of education
- Knowledge
- Family, relatives
- Attitudes, behavior
- Body experiences
- Children's games
- Professional education
- Sexuality

❑ Each biography forms the human being and stays actively alive; most of how everybody is living in the present time has been built up since the prenatal time.

❑ Psychological factors of development also belong to the biographical self-reflection, and this also since the prenatal time.

❑ Dealing with drives, needs and daily behavior is considerably formed within the first 10 years of life.

❑ The education of values and attitudes, also of religious and ideological beliefs, is based in the childhood and youth.

❑ Biographical self-reflection allows for a better understanding of the individual identity, of conflicts with oneself and life. Everybody can free themselves from 'burden' of the past and can also dissolve troublesome experiences through imagination and rational work on his own biography. This is an essential pre-condition for autonomy and freedom.

7.1. The Personal Life in Retrospect

Every human being has his own life biography. No two people have the same biography. The human being is not only a body with a psychical organism; he is also his individual vivid history. In a certain respect his past life is always also present and future.

Many people keep a diary; write letters to friends about events and their thoughts. Some draw or paint their experiences. We all take photos of impressive situations. So letters, photo albums and diaries are documents of the lived life. But also the living room tells us about life. Knick-knacks remind us of others or of special events. Paintings on the wall show the taste of the inhabitant and often point to the circumstances of the purchase. And above all clothes: People rarely buy their clothes accidentally. Influences are: habits assimilated from parents, stimulations from friends, suggestions from a current trend or model. It is similar with choosing a car, hobbies, etc.

We all remember moments, where our father or mother, grandfather or grandmother, an uncle or an aunt told us about experiences of their childhood. We remember when a teacher started with "That was a day when for the first time I...." - then it's immediately silent in the classroom.

Life histories are interesting, no matter if the story-teller wants to inflate his 'ego', or if he is touched by spontaneous memories, or if he simply wants to share his experiences with others.

We can all learn from the life history of others. But not only that: we start to understand the story-teller better. The one, who is telling about his life, feels lightened inside. So we can all participate in the life of others. In a group of regulars it may happen that everyone wants to tell their story and nobody wants to listen. Sometimes they only joke. Each one wants to talk of impressive experiences. Often they relate negative stories about others instead of their individual life; in order to cover up the shadows of their own life book.

People in love tell each other about their respective lives. That helps to form the relationship. One shares, demonstrates empathy, shares memories with one's partner, widens with one's own stories, comments and analyses, compares and judges, has questions and other solutions. In that way one becomes a lover of the other's life history.

We know: The biography forms the character and the self-identity. It influences health and daily activities.

Everybody sees life through the images of his life book and with the words of his learned communication.

The confrontation of one's own biography has a major value. By remembering we can elaborate the passed life and we can learn a lot. That is the way to acquire valuable knowledge about human life.

Reflections and Discussion

■ Some types of biographical communication formula from the everyday life are:

- "Do we know each other from somewhere?"
- "Have you lived here for a long time?"
- "Where have we come from?"
- "That was me at the time!"
- "At an earlier time I did it the same way."
- "Well, that's how it came about."
- "I have never felt so good before"
- "Tell me something about your life!"
- "Yes, the same thing happened to me."
- "You know, it was like that..."
- "You have never been through that!"
- "How times change!"
- "Exactly! How could I forget that?"
- "I won't put up with that."

■ Biographical aspects are:

• Sanctioned forms of living	• School
• Male and female roles	• Professional training and activities

▪ Health and disease	▪ Children's games
▪ Critical incidents	▪ Reading books
▪ Talents	▪ Military service
▪ Family system	▪ Ideologies, attitudes, mentality
▪ Experiences of role models	▪ Sociological conditions ('milieu')
▪ Forced self-denial	▪ Kinds of punishment and praise
▪ Neighborhood and peer group	▪ Manners as a basic experience of life

■ The life history of a person consists of a complex net with ramifications and connections.

- Body with health, nutrition, sexuality
- Work with professional training, activities, further education
- One's own family, parents, sisters, brothers, relatives
- School with education at all levels
- Religious education (people, rituals, subjects)
- Events such as festivities, quarrels, conflicts
- Acquaintances
- Leisure with all kind of activities
- Living area and environment
- Money, goods, insurances

■ Allegories to the biography of human beings are:

Life journey, tree of life, path of one's life, ship journey, traveling, fountain of youth, the life of Jesus, heroic epics, stories of the Grail, fairground, clockwork, trail, play, stage play, reincarnation, astrological structures of a course of life, examinations, mountain and valley trips, mountain climbing, etc.

Diagram 1.19: Biographical Network

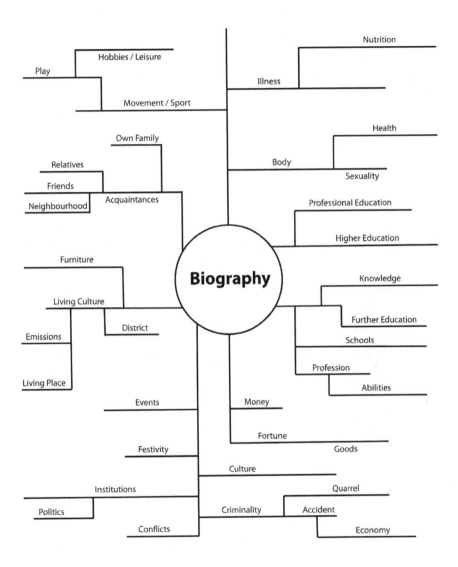

The Importance of the Biography

We understand the biography as an accumulation of experiences, acquired during the whole life process, which consciously or unconsciously goes into our activities. Experience means not only a cognitive dimension, but rather a holistic procedure which includes the body and the whole spectrum of sensual, preconscious, unconscious and rational potential... Biography is not an unhistorical, not-social 'private subject'; rather experiences are acquired in concrete historical and social contexts.

Human beings learn to understand why they act that way and not in another way, what influences social conditions had, how they dealt with those influences, and how these influences piled up in the individual biography and identity.

The life history of a human being is the history of scenic experiences (in the play of relationships), the personality is then the structure of these subjects of experiences, and the individuality of a human being is the unchangeable characteristic of this structure in a given social situation.

Earlier experiences are elaborated from the actual consciousness with actual forms, and as a result they receive a new quality. Each autobiographical document is, by its structure of time, the present past time and the remembered present (of the ego), and also a draft for the future. Remembering past concluded events allows the auto-biographer to (later) polish his life history, giving them a meaning afterwards by integrating and interpreting selected breakage, errors and bad experiences.

The memory firstly saves key-experiences from the life history, and only from that point of view can we recognize crucial lines between individual biography and collective history.

Biography makes destiny

Determination means to be determined to realize oneself. This contains: talent and dispositions, professional and spiritual commitments. 'Destiny' means in that context: the life environment to be at disposal and the psychical dispositions, formed by the biography. The acting forces are:

- The realities in the environment: delimitating possibilities for living
- Intuitive and psychodynamic attraction and repulsion (people, objects)
- The dynamic of development of all psychical forces and drives
- The intensity and dynamic of the defense mechanism and projection

- Ego-strength, self-management, way of living and skills for dealing with life
- The moral character and the characteristics of a person and his behavior
- The economical and social (family, relationships) possibilities for life
- The personal and institutional empowerment (reinforcement)
- The active energy of affinity (experiencing an inner existential similarity
- The inventory in the subconscious (complexes, experiences, etc.)
- The level of education (knowledge, skills, the formed psychical life in general)
- The power of the dreams, in case a person practices dream interpretation
- Incidents, especially if they occur in a synchronized manner to the situation of the person
- Wrong decisions and behavior, weaknesses, false evaluation, misinterpretation, etc.

Biographical Elaboration

With biographical reflection one can learn to understand, why one acted in a certain way and not in another, which influences contained social conditions, which people determined over ones psychical development, how one dealt with those influences (and how one deals with them today), and how one's biography and self-identity formed itself to a whole structure.

The first aim of the biographical self-reflection is the understanding of events and their influences.

The second vital aim of biographical self-reflection is the development of changing possibilities and perspectives of actions.

The third aim is the searching for and understanding of the psychical-spiritual being (the 'mystery of mankind') with the help of one's own biography.

The memory of passed events through new interpretation and selection of the remembered experiences allows for the posterior palliation of the life story, the mistakes and bad experiences. There is the possibility of deception, distortion and suppression.

That means: The human being would like to imagine a better life story. An 'ugly' biography strains the self image because the biography is somewhat always a part of what the person is. And mostly a human being wants to be more, that what he truly is.

The biographical self-reflection allows assimilating in a continuous process the pieces of the life history into the consciousness – everything that has been suppressed – and to step by step discover and understand the mosaic of what has become. One does not have the freedom to choose one's parents and frame of life.

What everyone becomes in their first 18 years of life underlies decisively the responsibility of the parents and the life environment (school, church, culture, etc.). Through biographical analysis and contemplation its critical content can be changed.

In the biographical analysis, previous experiences are worked out with the current state of consciousness. Therewith the lived biography gains a new quality. Through such reprocessing "life knowledge" is assimilated, also wisdom.

The analysis of the biography is also stocktaking of oneself. The confrontation with the own biography is also an attempt at explaining the changing and accumulating self images and self interpretations of life.

The levels of analysis in the auto-biography are:

- The objective level of the material, cultural and historical norms;
- The objective level of the events, incidents and actions;
- The psychical level of the experiences and occurrences;
- The psychical level of the reminiscence;
- The symbolic level of the linguistic presentation with vague and fragmentary memories.

In these processes of transformation, selection and reconstruction lays the possibility for trickery, deformation and suppression, but also a possibility for information and correction.

Education is the answer and the suggestion of the pedagogical reflections about epochal problem situations, experienced as 'crises.

Self-education creates and transforms one's own biography and with that also the person, the way of living and their future perspectives!

Notes and Perspectives

What purpose does biographical elaboration and analysis serve in everyday life?

Write down the central keywords from this sub-chapter:

What is the human being without reflecting about his lived life?

Explain: Biographical elaboration is important because…:

What did people learn about the importance of the biography in their parent's home, at school and in the church?

What importance does biographical elaboration have in the communication between life partners and in the interactions in general?

How do the people in politics and the economy show their biography?

What does advertising convey to us about the importance of the biography?

Formulate an important question about biographical reflection:

7.2. Forming Psychical Forces in the Life Course

The psychical forces start to be formed already in the prenatal time. They later determine the life course. The fetus reacts to the voice of the mother, of the father and the emotional environment of the parents. First patterns of reaction are formed.

The baby inside the mother's womb is capable of communicating kinetically. The birth has a decisive psychological influence on the new-born baby: From the sensual joy to the uterine contraction, then through parturition into the glaring light.

And then the 'reception': welcome? Not welcome? This leaves traces on the memory. Reactions to the stimuli from the environment start to form. Reflexes are built up: screaming, sucking, sleeping, scrambling, withdrawing, clasping, being attentive, moving and interpreting signals.

During the early childhood characteristics are formed: active searching, discovering, crying, smiling, assimilating stimuli from the environment, reactions of separation, being shy with strangers, playing, stability of relation, patterns of behavior to activate interesting reactions and many more.

Experiences of lust start to form patterns: drinking, eating, touching, drives, sexual pre-lust, punishing etc. These are the basic biographical experiences, the psychical foundation of the development of life. During childhood the forming of the concrete-operational and formal thinking starts. This goes on until the end of youth.

More and more self-experiences and abilities develop through the family home, school and leisure activities. Self-identity is formed strongly through sexual maturity and sexual distinction. Patterns of thought and the role of the parents are deeply influential, manifold imitated. More and more is accumulated: images of God, religious rituals, attitudes to certain types of human beings and political groups.

The emotional dependence on the parents is set to move and change. The relationships with people of the same age become more mature. Sexual experiences with oneself form attitudes and experiences, in the context of sexual enlightenment and education. Leisure, performance, sport and body experiences also form the self-identity. Images about professional life create the foundation.

During that time the first intimate contacts begin in relationships with the opposite sex. All these processes of development form the individual biography. With the start of adulthood all psychical forces are considerably formed. The repertoire of behavior for all kinds of life situations even has a habitual dynamism.

The economic position within the professional life and the social incorporation stays in the foreground, among friendships, love relationships and plans for marital life or family (or for a 'single-life').

It is time to discover more about life: nowadays, overall through journeys. The life plan is drafted more and more elaborately: life shall grow like a tree; or left to grow wild like bushes. The formed psychical forces determine the course.

Reflections and Discussion

■ Childhood and youth are not only a section of life, which can be checked off for success or failure, just to turn towards the future and 'freedom'. In this phase of the life course the foundations for the whole life are formed.

Decisive forming factors are:

▪ Affirmation / negation of pregnancy	▪ Religious education, experiences
▪ Emotional environment before birth	▪ Environment of the same age-group
▪ Free space for individual discovering	▪ Stimuli for soul and reason
▪ Acceptance of one's own abilities	▪ Consumption: practice in the family
▪ People who are considered to be examples	▪ Kinds of leisure activities
▪ Economical situation of the parents	▪ Expectations of performances and offers
▪ Educational environment in the family	▪ Experiences of love and hatred
▪ School (and teacher) experiences	▪ Experiences about quarrels / conflicts
▪ Body self-experiences (prohibitions)	▪ Disposition of the parents

■ Drives, needs and behavior patterns are being practiced:

■ Lust of the body	■ Speaking	■ Consumption
■ Sexuality	■ Listening	■ Relationships
■ Tenderness	■ Desire for knowledge	■ Roles in the housework
■ Eating	■ Defense mechanism	■ Roles of work place
■ Drinking	■ Values	■ Roles in groups
■ Sleeping	■ Attitudes	■ Reactions to illness
■ Relaxation	■ Beliefs	■ Psychical reactions
■ Curiosity for discovering	■ Interest in culture	■ Power behavior

■ Each adult deals differently with his daily experiences according to his first life phase. With increasing age human beings become more and more different, manifold, complex and individual. There is a large variety in the kind and amount of life experiences. The biography develops in this abundance of individually given facts.

Some keywords to this scope of experiences:

■ Different relationships	■ Illnesses, accidents, victim of events
■ Political education	■ Money (that means life possibilities)
■ Professional development	■ Offending experiences
■ Blows of destiny	■ Success and failure
■ Path of one's own family (children)	■ Professional satisfaction

Diagram 1.20: Steps of Development in the Biography

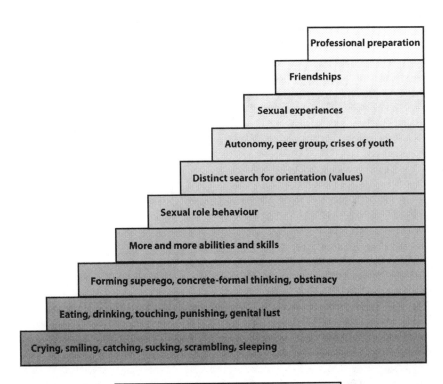

Professional preparation

Friendships

Sexual experiences

Autonomy, peer group, crises of youth

Distinct search for orientation (values)

Sexual role behaviour

More and more abilities and skills

Forming superego, concrete-formal thinking, obstinacy

Eating, drinking, touching, punishing, genital lust

Crying, smiling, catching, sucking, scrambling, sleeping

Humanistic Development:

Self-determination and autonomy
Process-being and inner deepening
Self-identity and self-confidence
Spontaneity and creativity
Experiences of transcendency

Life Course under Psychical Aspects

Biographical self-reflection is important, also within the context of the phases of psychical development: The existentially missed childhood burdens not only the youth, but the adulthood and also the human life. The same applies to puberty, adolescence and virility. The human being is constantly in a process of 'becoming'. This 'becoming' is carried out in contest with oneself and the surrounding environment.

Three anthropological set-ups to the biographical self-reflection:

1) The personality of human beings characterized by uniqueness and put to being with others
2) That the human being is steadily growing (becoming)
3) That this growth (becoming) is not only an endogen guided process, but also happening in interaction with the environment

The ordinary pattern of the life course of an adult:

1) The early adult-age is marked by the readiness through testing and through vitality.
2) In the first part of the middle adult-age the roles of adults and responsibility are consolidated.
3) After that follows, in the second part of the middle adult-age, a call to question duties; and (then) a reintegration.
4) In each of these phases there exists a connection between the individual, the familiar and the professional development.

It's always relative what an adult is: There are for example enough young people between the age of 20 and 30, who we wouldn't regard as 'adult'. If we take the adults after the age of 65, as the final-point of the adult-age, we enter into more difficulties. Some retire, some become unable to do business, others remain as efficient as at 55. Some theses:

1) It is proved, that the order of life phases varies considerably by intercultural comparison and in the historical process.
2) The development to modern life is a process of life time organization, away from statically organized life forms.
3) There is today a standard normal course of life.
4) There is also a large process of individualization that means liberation of (earlier) corporative and local links.
5) The life course is organized around the professional (business) life, in three phases: preparation, business and retirement.

Each society has an order of ages, has formal and informal norms for every life period. The environment reacts with judgment on deviation, with resentment or acceptance. The human being is considered as creator of his development. He is understood as a recognizing and self-reflecting species, who has an image about himself and his environment, and who modifies both, in the course of evaluation of old and new experiences.

At the base of all reactions (of the human being/the psychic apparatus) remains not the contradiction of love and hate, nor the Eros and Death instinct, but the contradiction of ego (person, id=lust-ego) and external world... for that reason the first reaction of each creature must be a striving for contact with the external world. That means: Human development - and with that the biography - stays always in the instinctive contact with the ego and the external world.

Phases of Biographical Development

Inferiority is a driving force of the human development. A feeling of inferiority arises from the constitutional inferiority and from similar acting positions in childhood, which demand compensation, with the purpose of increasing the feeling of personality. With that the fictive final purpose of striving for power receives an enormous influence and pushes all psychical forces in its direction (A. Adler). At the beginning of each soul-life there is a more or less deep feeling of inferiority. That is the driving force, the point, from which all desires of a child start and develop, to set a goal from which he expects all the calm and security of his life for the future. (A. Adler)

The 3-phases-model of Sigmund Freud seems to manage the whole biography of humans:

- The oral phase (1st year): take in, hold on, bite, spit out, close;
- 2nd phase: the anal phase (2nd and 3rd year): hold back, cleanness, pass and excrete, perform (present), give, play with excrement;
- The phallic phase (3rd to 6th year): search, penetrate and take possession.

For C. G. Jung the biography is divided into two phases: The process of 'initiation into the external world' until the middle of one's life and after the 'initiation into the inner world'.

The Psychoanalyst Erik Erikson presents a model from the inner point of view:

1. (Early infancy): Confidence against distrust
2. (Baby age): Autonomy against shame, doubt
3. (Play-age): Initiative against feelings of guilt
4. School age: Sense of working against feeling of inferiority
5. (Adolescence): Identity and rejection against diffusion of identity
6. (Early adult-age): Intimacy and solidarity against isolation
7. (Adult age): Reproduction (Integration) or rejection (to live, to create, and to care)
8. (Mature adult age): Integrity against desperation

Human beings never pass through a psychical development, which is conditioned only by biological processes. The psychical process is always defined through learning and thinking processes. These change with the years. Development is not a process which ends with childhood or youth; rather it lasts the whole life. Psychical development can be described by the following four characteristics:

1. Differentiation and refinement;
2. Centralization: building up a higher central authority which works as a steering function.
3. Stabilization, canalization (increasing limitation of the possibilities)
4. Active creation (the human being determines, through his decisions at a given moment with a certain measure, also his future decisions.

The problems of learning and psychological development are formed through dealing with some or all of the following basic situations:

1. Situations of professional and economic competition;
2. Situations of the family;
3. Becoming aware of the insufficiency of one's individual existence;
4. Friction about the monotony of the individual existence;
5. Becoming aware of the finality of the individual destiny;
6. Confrontation with the finiteness of existence.

Notes and Perspectives

What purpose does the reflection about the own psychological development of the life course serve?

Write down the central keywords from this sub-chapter:

What is the human being without reflection about the forming factors in his life course?

Explain: A humanistic development is important because…:

What did people learn about forming the psychical forces in the life course in their parent's home, at school and in the church?

What importance does the humanistic development have in the communication between life partners and in the interactions in general?

How do politics and the economy understand the humanistic development of the human beings?

What does advertising convey to us about the forming factors of the environment?

Formulate an important question about humanistic development:

7.3. History about Formation of Values and Attitudes

The social life is considerably directed by norms, as customs, as law or rules. The whole life - contacts, relationships, activities, purchase and sale - is full of norms, founded in each case by judgments: 'That is good', or 'That is bad' and consequently: 'You are allowed to do that' or 'You must do that'.

We can't live without social norms. Everybody adopts such norms in his early childhood. Autonomy increases with the beginning of the age of 10. Children ask: "Why do I have to do that?"

Norms represent values and those again are embedded in arguments, in a system of philosophical or religious attitudes and beliefs. One's own biography is considerably defined by the adopted system of values. And that doesn't just happen by accident.

It may be a coincidence that Fritz is born into a Catholic family, Anna into a Protestant family and Omar into an Islamic family. Basic attitudes towards life are somehow already there, when a child takes his place in that family.

Human beings value themselves and others, the life and the transcendence (religion), whether they want it or not, primarily due to biographical experiences.

In fact the value systems in a pluralistic society are manifold. But a child can't choose his values and norms like toy in a toy shop. However, each young adult forms his own values; the forming of the conscious is deeply engraved through parents, school and others. Biographical self-reflection demands a thorough elaboration of this conditioning.

In the beginning there is authority (after Sigmund Freud the relationship to the father; obedience and punishment), then the individual needs, then the people in the environment, then the state and religion, and finally utilitarian considerations: justice and dignity shall receive values.

Only very few people deal with that beyond deep philosophical arguments about values and beliefs. And even less people are ready to engage themselves in the higher values of the human being such as dignity and justice.

The individual biography always decisively contributes to determining how somebody values, judges and lives.

216

We can notice this in all daily interests like communication and manners, or in dealing with capital subjects like sexuality, marriage, environment, death penalty, termination of pregnancy, violence, religious beliefs, war etc.

If 'God' or 'pleasure and joy' remains the major aim, it is rarely a result of one's own thoughts. More-over some have the 'true God', while others say, that those have only a got 'partial truth of God'. In the end there is violence and war; or, if they are free from dogmas: Humanity and wisdom.

Reflections and Discussion

■ There are different possibilities to justify values and norms; some examples:

■ Pleasure and joy of life	■ Freedom of will and responsibility
■ Consequences of responsibility	■ Individual interests, general well-being
■ Fortune, happiness	■ The good life
■ Freedom as the highest value	■ Laws of God
■ Natural talents as a basic argument	■ To realize the psychical life
■ Good and bad will (with reasoning)	■ Principles of Individuation

■ Word combination made with 'value':

■ Good	■ Changing	■ Ideal
■ Religious	■ Good ideals	■ Spiritual
■ Humanistic	■ Realistic	■ Aesthetic
■ Economical	■ Utility	■ Other world
■ Comparing	■ Intrinsic	■ Judgment
■ Freedom	■ Pleasure	■ Absolute

■ Terms of values are:

▪ Good	▪ Ugly	▪ Holy	▪ Right
▪ Evil	▪ Disgusting	▪ Negative	▪ Idiotic
▪ Bad	▪ Sublime	▪ Positive	▪ Admirable
▪ Abominable	▪ Harmonic	▪ Exemplary	▪ Dignified
▪ Beautiful	▪ Crafty	▪ Wrong	▪ Diabolic

■ It is helpful to recognize the different structure of sentences by the judgments:

a) Moral judgment of obligation:

▪ You shouldn't have sex before you get married
▪ Love is a duty for everybody
▪ You should practice self-knowledge

b) Moral judgment of values:

▪ You have a highly valuable character
▪ My father is a bad man
▪ He has miserable motives for his behavior

c) Non-moral judgments of values:

▪ That's a beautiful car
▪ My parents didn't have a good life
▪ Christianity is the best religion

Diagram 1.21: Moral Education and its Critical Aspects

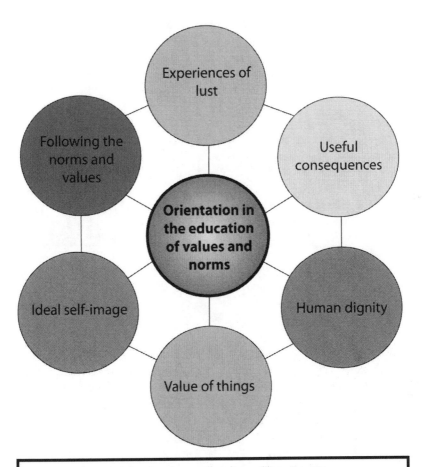

For critical orientation in self-reflection:
- Formulation of values and norms
- Relativity of values against indoctrination
- Highest values of human beings and daily values
- Preconditions of developmental psychology
- Values and the effects of values
- Moral hipocrisy
- Hidden values in the unconscious

Morality as a Biographical Result

The super-ego represents the social norms, on the one hand from the conscious, on the other hand from the ego-ideal. This contains the laws and prohibitions of the parents (the representation of the relationship with the parents), especially with the father, but also of role models and authorities (religion, moral and social sense). The super-ego puts on the strongest yardstick. In other words: The education of the conscious and values is built up from birth through the relationship with the parents.

The power of the super-ego: Much talk about 'self-determination', 'self-realization', 'autonomy', 'maturity' and 'emancipation' cannot camouflage that most people in the highly industrialized societies succumb to external guidance. The need for the acceptance of others pulls with a strong feeling of dependency and an extraordinary readiness to receive and follow the actions and desires of others, above all public opinion. In this psychical state almost nobody risks putting forward a proposal for himself or for others about principles of morals and norms which goes further than the vague common interest, or even which is contradictory to it.

Another aspect: The values become norms which want to be realized. They push to become, starting from a first un-individual state, a state of subjective possession.

The 'rigorous super-ego': The words of Kant, that we are cultivated and civilized, more than onerously, but still far away from moral education, are confirmed by the events of the 20th century: civil wars, tribal wars, wars for expansion, race wars, race fanaticism, ideological and prestige-bound wars, disregard for human rights, thousand-fold tortures, hundred-thousand-fold deaths through wars, exodus, hundred-thousand-fold misery and death through ideological fanaticism. What is the value of human life today? The dark sides: Nobody can count how many human beings were maltreated, abused, hurt or killed during history.

Only those can learn virtue and can develop morality, who try to transform their own reasoning into action, with the best of one's knowledge and belief, and from that belief arises integrity. We need people today with 'backbone', with moral courage.

Moral education has to lead to a holistic program for the development of personality and for social competences; moral education shouldn't be limited to thinking-training, but also has to promote a moral sensibility and a moral capacity of behavior.

Characteristics of the 'Postmodern' influence today the life course of human beings. Some key-words: mixing of things and ideas (from everything and everybody), side by side and disorder of fiction and facts; no limits between culture, business, consumption and production; cultural values are not just spiritualized, but have to be brought to men and women through marketing and promotion. One is shifting the importance of the content from a statement to the package.

If there is a lack of being affected and a lack of individual obligation, then the risk arises, that morality becomes abstract and ultimately sterile. If the individual feelings and values are over-accentuated, or more precisely: if they don't depend on knowledge and reasoning and if they are not guided from inside, then the over-individual nature of morality and the feeling for a real obligation gets lost.

The core of immorality consists of not wanting to know, making oneself blind to one's own knowledge, and overdoing it in actions.

Revision of Morality

Some stimulating ideas (exercises) about religion and political ideologies:

Aim: to become aware of ideologies and prejudices, with which we were confronted in the course of our life and to think about the influences of such ideologies on our attitudes and our behavior. Starting sentences are:

▪ Politicians are...	▪ Most important in life is...
▪ Communists are...	▪ To your parents you should...
▪ Somebody is educated who...	▪ Boys should...
▪ He, who performs something, is...	▪ Girls should...
▪ Money and properties are...	▪ Towards bosses you should...
▪ As a good Christian...	▪ Women should take care of...
▪ Life is...	▪ Towards strangers you should...

Aim: Presentation and visualization of one's own religiousness and of the course of relations to the church until today: "...". The exercise is an imagination.

Aim: Going through one's own ideas about God, from childhood until today. The exercise is again an imagination: Think about God. Remember how you imagined Him as a child; think about experiences, fantasies, problems you had with God during your life course, etc.

Aim: To clarify the influences on the origin and change of political attitudes in one's own biography: Aspects for rational reflections in hindsight are:

- Attitudes of the parents, of relatives...
- Experiences with political events...
- Influences from movies, television, school, political groups...
- Influences from same-age people, from friends, from the newspapers...

Human beings are living in the past much more then we are aware of. The main reason is: We interpret the reality with concepts and ideologies, which we base on past experiences.

As adolescents we construct our interpretations of the reality around defined words. That is why we orientate ourselves with old maps:

1) Human beings create the world ... and they are created by the world ... education is a part of the human development...

2) The human kind of living becomes a result of the cultural formation ... the development of humanity and coming nearer to being fit human beings doesn't follow natural evolution.

3) Education stays between reflection and action ... education is based on the responsibility of each of us.

The biography starts in the prenatal time. A human being has a much greater chance of becoming an emotionally stable adult, if his mother is happily looking forward to the birth.

→ To consider: Each morality includes emotional components.

Notes and Perspectives

What purpose does the reflection about the own moral education serve?

Write down the central keywords from this sub-chapter:

What is the human being without a reflected moral education?

Explain: Reflection about what people have learnt and from the environment adapted moral education is important because…:

What did people learn about the subjectivity and relativity of the moral education in their parent's home, at school and in the church?

What importance does the education of norms and values have in the communication between life partners and in the interactions in general?

How do politics and the economy promote a critical reflection about the education of values and moral?

What does advertising convey to us about the education of values and moral?

Formulate an important question about the reflection about education of values and moral:

7.4. Exercises

1. What are the people's attitudes towards their past life?
2. Looking back, which part of their life will they have few or vague memories of?
3. a) Which memories do people deal with rather badly?
3. b) Which memories do people deal with rather well?
3. c) How do people experience the fact that their biography is the coding for their present?
3. d) How do people realize that their way of living today is programming their future?

4. Note to each of the 20 fields of subjects 1 outstanding characteristic a majority of people do not like to remember.

4.1. Family: Parents, Stepparents, brothers and sisters, relatives, style of education, formation, work, social conditions, absences (separation, death)
4.2. Relationships out of the family: acquaintances, neighbors, work colleagues, priests, doctors, counselors, teachers, ethnic groups
4.3. Friendships, love relationships, marriage
4.4. Own family, children, the family of the partner, patterns of relationship
4.5. Living, living atmosphere, quality of living and the surrounding, moving
4.6. Body, sexuality, sex education, being man / woman, the culture in the bathroom, pregnancy (course, termination), menstruation
4.7. Nutrition, culture of eating and drinking
4.8. Illnesses, disturbances, suffering, operation, therapy, addiction (alcohol, tobacco, medicines, drugs, eating, playing)
4.9. Pre-school, school, further education, learning, education, subjects, certificates, change of school, school career
4.10. Professional formation, working, work activities, workplace, unemployment

4.11. Leisure places and activities, hobbies, games, holidays, weekends, mobility

4.12. Religious practices, belief, philosophy of life, esoteric, sects, psycho-religious movements (organizations)

4.13. Political socialization, political events, activities, ecological movements

4.14. Cultural life, reading (newspaper, magazines, books), music, art, film, theatre, television

4.15. Objects, articles of consumption, clothes, money, items of values

4.16. Psycho-social Institutions: unemployment insurance, public welfare, counseling, social work centers, homes, insurance benefit

4.17. House work, life administration (e.g. taxes, insurances)

4.18. Sleeping (environment, habits, dreams)

4.19. Criminality (victim, actor)

4.20. Ecological environment: air and water pollution, traffic, noise, overpopulation, poverty, rubbish, cruelty to animals, consumption of energy, catastrophes, violence, riots, war

Multiple Choice Test

Choose the four correct answers and mark them with a cross: ☒ a) lust

7.1. Which are the central biographical aspects for self-reflection?

☐ a) Environment (milieu)
☐ b) Health, illness
☐ c) Aunts, uncles
☐ d) Children's games
☐ e) Critical events
☐ f) Father's cooking skills

7.2. For the biography of everybody the following psychical factors of development are decisive:

☐ a) The anal phase
☐ b) Being a good pupil
☐ c) Lust of discovering
☐ d) Calm times
☐ e) Development of integrity
☐ f) Testing the physical forces

7.3. The subject 'moral education in the life course' allows the following to be formulated:

☐ a) Moral formation starts from the moment of the earliest memories.
☐ b) Moral education starts to be an act of thinking during adolescence.
☐ c) Everybody experiences through education and training the most important, valid for all people, true values.
☐ d) 'That is a good vacuum cleaner' is a non-moral judgment of value.
☐ e) Not many people reflect on their systems of values and beliefs.
☐ f) The processes of transformation and the phases of Individuation can be experienced and are a constructive orientation in the essential values of life.

8. Health and Stress

Health and 'mental fitness' are manifested in the life style, and also in the way of dealing with problems; thus: Mental fitness is important for well-being in the psychical and social life.

Essential Theses

❑ A good body experience (feeling) can be built up, for example with:

- Nature experience
- Control feelings
- Moderation in all
- Correct nutrition
- Healthy attitudes
- Self-responsibility
- Stress balance
- Relaxation
- Sexuality

❑ The relation to one's own body and the state of the body are developed also through the individual biography. To consciously experience body and sensuality and to care for them increases health.

❑ Everybody can develop a life style for health and well-being and live it creatively.

❑ 'Health' includes more then a 'healthy functioning of the body'; it includes the whole human being with his psychical-spiritual and social being.

❑ To an individual life style belongs: movement, nutrition, nature experience, decorating living areas, dealing with others, leisure activities etc.

❑ Mental fitness means on the one hand thinking, including perception and watchfulness. On the other hand intuition, imagination and spiritual experiences are also part of it.

❑ Mental fitness has a decisive function in all personal and professional areas for satisfaction, success, fulfillment and happiness. Mental fitness is open for all challenges of life, from inside and also from outside.

8.1. Body Experiences and Sensuality

Nothing goes without the body and senses. We know: The psyche influences the body; and vice versa. The state of the body influences the psychical life. Somebody who is hungry is often in a bad mood, nervous and unsatisfied. Eating too much makes vitality sluggish.

The suppression of sexual lust causes many psycho-somatic diseases and social conflicts. Too much fat is fattening; too much alcohol overstrains the liver; a lack of dietary fiber makes the bowels inert; too much sugar irritates the intestinal flora; a lack of exercise weakens the heart; too much salt... smoking too much... too much noise..., etc.

Everybody experiences his body in some way or another; some positively, others with rather negative feelings. We must care for our body: nutrition, clothes and movements. If we do that unreasonably, it has consequences for which we all are jointly liable. The costs are high! We can learn how to build up a healthy life style. Individual responsibility is essential.

We live with the senses: We eat with the eyes; we like to see colors; we are moved by sound and clothes; we react to touch, to tenderness. We experience nature with senses; while we eat we smell, taste and perceive the atmosphere; we discover the world with body movements; we don't only smell perfume, but also entire life situations; we work with posture; we speak and quarrel with the whole body, etc.

It seems that a certain self-education can only be an advantage. Everybody takes with him, his biography, as well as innumerable habits from the environment. We eat in as we did in the early childhood, or we realize our sensuality the way our education has formed it.

Few people learn how important the experiences of the senses are. Nowadays we hear more about that through the media; we are even strongly sensually influenced. But what do we do for our health education - sensual, physical, psychical, social and ecological?

We can learn to reflect and to improve our way of living concerning the body, also recognizing biographical conditioning. As a lot of physical and psychical illnesses are conditioned by the biography, so is the right way of living the 'product' of education and alien influences. We can form our perception for physical needs. We can learn to please with our senses. Well-being is a source of life force.

In the physical posture we recognize psychical life. Body movements can be slack or dynamic, tenacious or flowing, harmonious or 'abrupt', like a heavy or light load, aggressive or calm-pleasant, hesitant or even impulsive.

We experience body movements and body shapes as beautiful and harmonious or ugly and clumsy. Clothes contribute to well-being and to movements: confined, liberating, lustful, compulsory or ritualized.

→ For all that the education of using the senses is essential for our health.

Reflections and Discussion

■ The state of the body and the relation with one's own body contribute decisively to psychical well-being; characteristics of this are for example:

• Creative forces	• Adapting to stress	• Balance
• Realistic aims	• Healthy self-acceptation	• Interest in life
• Humanistic values	• Autonomy	• Social openness
• Fulfilling basic needs	• Stability	• Dealing with aggression

■ Everybody experiences his body, healthy or ill, with lust or un-lust:

• Skin	• Hands, fingers	• Sexual organs	• Kidneys
• Tensions	• Legs	• Mouth	• Heart
• Muscles	• Stomach, abdomen	• Hair	• Breathing organs

■ We experience our body as:

Slack	Tense	Fresh	Cozy	Worn-out
Beautiful	Stiff	Tired	Lustful	Plump clumsy
Ugly	Relaxed	Exhausted	Nauseous	Tenacious
Vital	Nervous	Pleasant	Aversive	Embarrassing
Forceful	Heavy	Unpleasant	Cold	Joyless
Harmonious	Light	Disgusting	Sour	Intensive

■ We can build up a good body feeling:

▪ Nature experience	▪ Correct nutrition	▪ Massage	▪ Herbs, oils
▪ Light sport, walking	▪ Measure in all	▪ Physical love	▪ Interest in the biological life
▪ Nature experience	▪ Relaxation training	▪ Healthy attitudes	▪ Healthy environment
▪ Meditation	▪ Self-responsibility	▪ Eating habits	▪ Cooking
▪ Stress-management	▪ Correct nutrition	▪ Culture of living	▪ Lustful positive care of the body
▪ Reduction of quarrels	▪ Mental-training	▪ Culture of clothes	▪ Self-esteem

■ Many people are forced into risky habits through their biography and through their environment, for example:

- Denying: love, truthfulness, loyalty, solidarity, higher values...
- Social pressure: imitating, need for acceptance, popular images...

Diagram 1.22: Holistic Health and Beig Safe

9 Points for Holistic Health

1. Saying 'yes' to life, positive relation to the body
2. Life-skills through elaboration and education
3. Constructive relations to masculinity and femininity
4. Capacity for elaboration and burden
5. Educating (forming) of the individual potentials
6. Strive for humanity, meanings and values
7. Spirituality and its integration into life
8. Care for the ecological environment
9. Realization of the archetypal procedures

Thesis about Health and Illness:

The highest meaning and value of human beings
doesn't consist in the totality of the health
of the body and the psyche.

The way of living through Individuation
with its areas of experience and actions
- body, psyche, social and ecological environment,
nature and animals - creates, that what
'being safe' means.

The Term 'Health'

What is health?

Health is defined according to the World Health Organization (WHO): "... as a complete bodily, psychical and social well-being and not only as the absence of illness and disease."

- A definition about 'health': "Health is a culture of all life means; health is assimilation of body and environment through social actions; health is a path which is formed by going along it."

- Factors of health are also methodical principles such as 'aspire for appropriateness', 'respond to feelings', 'nearness to life'.

- Seven activities for health promote health and avoid illness: 'no (moderate) smoking', 'moderate alcohol', 'moderate fat with the right composition', 'calculated need of calories', 'moderate salt (5-6 gr.)', 'managing stress' and 'balance the lack of movements'.

- Self-responsibility and self-determination are valued as an important part of a healthy personality development.

- Health is understood as a part of the individual life course development, as a process which is only possible, if an individual manages flexibly and aimed at the time the best reachable state of coordination of inner and external requirements, ensuring a satisfactory continuity of the self-experience (self-identity).

- Health is related to a high capacity of adaptability of human beings to physical, psychical and social burden and the entire way of living.

- Practical aspects: Training of perception or sensitization means to develop a bigger sensitivity, precision and differentiation for inner and external proceedings. Perception and creating, impression and expression come full circle. They influence each other.

- Intensity and diversity of perceptions and their individual elaboration are one of the preconditions for a creative forming. Holistic perception comes from the harmonious interplay of sensual and spiritual (mental) forces.

Health and education:

Health-education is understood as an effort to build up an individual, correct healthy way of living which includes social, economic and ecological points of view of human behavior. Responsible behavior-patterns in the sense of health-education aim at widening the individual behavior-skills in a concrete socio-cultural life area with its requests, given elements and free spaces.

We can say the same to illness, nutrition, movements and clothing. They are also biographically conditioned. To become aware is a precondition to creating a program for an individual correct healthy behavior.

An example: The essential questions about eating are: When? What? How much? Where? How? How long? Why? With? Who has prepared the food?

Similar questions can be put in the frame of a report or in a biographical reflection about movements, clothing and other experiences.

→ Organism and psyche (mind) are connected with the social and physical environment.

Aspects of Psychical Health

A list of factors from psychological and psychoanalytical theories about psychical health; the following statements are resumed and freely formulated:

- Productivity, creativity, being active, working interest
- The objective-rational contact with the reality
- Adaptability
- Internal balance, ego-integration
- Ability to satisfy needs
- Genital sexuality
- Being free from (or limited) use of defense mechanism
- Tolerance of frustration, control of impulses, strengthened against stress
- Power of resistance against psychical illness
- Being free of symptoms
- Realistic definition of aims
- Balance between dependency and independency
- Balance between stability and flexibility
- Basic confidence
- Ego-identity, realistic self-image
- Realization of individual potentials
- Autonomy and resistance against enculturation

- Self-responsibility
- Autonomous morality
- Self-understanding
- Self-acceptance, self-esteem, and self-confidence
- Naturalness, being free of facades, spontaneity, sociability, genuineness
- Openness for experiences and feelings
- Experiences of transcendence, 'positive feelings'
- Mind-expanding
- Acceptance of one's own body
- Aiming at the 'good', the truth, the beauty
- Humor
- Democratic character-structure
- Need for privacy
- Orientation in meaning and values
- Ability to a constructive mastering of suffering
- Will-power

This list makes it obvious that health means much more than 'absence of illnesses'. Health isn't something someone has or not, that we can lose and gain back. Health also isn't something, that is added to the human life and that can make life more beautiful and more comfortable. Health is a manner of living, is realization of life, and is a way of mastering life.

Usual and known is the system of risk-factors. To those factors we contrast the constructive factors for health: Those allow us to experience health in each stage and moment as something which feels good, that motivates us from itself to more effort for health, and improves the healthy self-initiative and self-responsibility.

These are for example:

- nutrition, breathing, movements, sleeping
- temperature, care for, love, safety, security
- pleasant experiences, reason, intelligence
- self-control, internalization, meditation
- experiences of transcendence
- a life rhythm suited to the organism

Notes and Perspectives

What purpose does holistic health serve?

Write down the central keywords from this sub-chapter:

What is the human being without psychical health?

Explain: Psychical health is important because…:

What did people learn about holistic health in their parent's home, at school and in the church?

What importance does psychical health have in the communication between life partners and in the interactions in general?

How seriously do politics and the economy take the holistic health?

What does advertising convey to us about psychical health?

Formulate an important question about holistic health:

8.2. Lifestyle for Health and Well-being

We live in difficult times with challenges which have never existed before: consumption, prosperity (poverty next-door), comfort and large variety of experiences. A view of the Earth with joy of life on the sofa! Human beings are spoiled. Can we blame anybody? Generally we surely can't.

The external pressure is enormous: even small stimuli activate sexual lust, romantic fantasies, aggressive feelings, the desire to eat, the need to drink and much more. The single human beings drown in the intricate mass of information and consumption. We can get more and more with less and less effort.

Everything is achievable with money. Or what is not? For those who 'have', life is neither hard, nor strenuous, nor arduous, nor is it full of deprivations. 'Pleasure without effort' is the motto. But then people lose their original identity, their self-being, their inner autonomy, their integrity, their psychical-spiritual maturity and their well-being.

We can create a creative and autonomous life style, open for growth, only with an extensive self-education. That means: an individual culture with oneself in the private living sphere and in the environment of leisure. To a life style we include: eating and drinking habits; patterns of mobility and modalities of movements (lack of movements); genuineness of experiences (experience of nature); concentrated self-management in all daily matters; style of communication and care for relationships etc.

Health means more than 'physical well-being', more than 'psychical well-being'; health includes a genuine identity, inner authenticity, realization (to give expression) of inner talents, ability to control instinct and drive-satisfaction, also ability for love. Health thus means a form of being and of living. This is for everybody a 'product' of his biography and his reflections about that.

The aims of self-education are not the exact calculation of calories, the amount of salt, of fat or alcohol per day etc.; these are building-stones in the complex networked system of human life.

Life style and life culture become an expression of the individual growth in the process of Individuation. Care for health here isn't just an added element.

Self-reflexive questions about the individual life culture are for example: How do I eat? How 'mobile' am I with and without a car?

How do I speak (on the phone and everywhere)? How do I choose my clothes and shoes? How do I experience my home? How do I create love and sexual lust? How do I do my house work? How do I manage my money? How do I chose and create being together with others? How do I handle waste? How do I manage information? How seriously do I take my physical needs?

The being forced to create the personal life, networked with human beings, biography and environment, becomes the meaning of an individual human growth. This demands a critical self-reflection. This is the basis for happiness and well-being.

Reflections and Discussion

■ It is difficult to create an individual life style for health and well-being. Many external influences and also the biographical conditions, set limitations:

Flood of information (Media)	Immense book market	Leisure offers
Images in advertisements	'Zeitgeist'	Fashion trends
Classical career patterns	Social pressure everywhere	Habits from youth
Examples from parents	Consumption	Stages and scenery

■ The following essentially belong to health:

Physical well-being	Ability for relationship	Experience of meaning
Ability for performance	Autonomy, inner freedom	Creative abilities
Self-reflection	Balance	Balance of stress
Psychical 'going round'	Tolerance of frustration	Self-realization
Elaborated biography	Being free of symptoms	Satisfaction of needs
Ability of will	Integrity	Hope

- Critical self-reflection to an individual life style includes:

  - Do I feel well in my body?
  - Can I accept physical experiences, enjoy lust and create lust?
  - Which reaction do I have to house work and how do I do it?
  - How consciously do I dress and buy my clothes?
  - How and with which aims do I furnish (decorate) my home?
  - How and with what attitudes do I care for my body?
  - How do I handle the media and how do I behave in front of the television?
  - How do I decorate and experience my bedroom, and my kitchen?
  - How do I treat food and how do I choose my nutrition?
  - What do I allow for myself? When? Why? How?
  - How do I keep company with others?

- Autonomy and freedom increase with decisions for certain values and kinds of living:

  - What is important for me personally in my every day life?
  - Which values do I live purposefully with decision and concentration?
  - How do I maintain my limits towards others (e.g. visits)?
  - How do I accept stimulations from others and therefore widen my so-being?

Diagram 1.23: Stress and Precuations

Stressors:
Noise, odors, emissions, acid rain, poisons
Dense population, narrow places, crowds
Pressure of prestige and success, performance ambition
Frustration, worries, conflicts, anxiety, anger, rage
Wrong nutrition, lack of movement, few nature experiences
Lie, cheat, distrust, living masks

Stress Reactions:
Body, organs, senses, sleep, calm
Sexuality, relationships, experience of needs
Communication, learning, actions
Eating, drinking, movements, nature experience

Health
Being Safe

Measures to deal with:
To train the capacity of burden
To increase the working through
To train the self-management
Relaxation and meditation
Working thorugh the biography
Decide for values of life
Life philosphy and wisdom
Life style with creativity

Stress and Stress Reactions

- Stress is a non specific physical reaction of the body to any given requirement.
- Stress isn't just a nervous tension.
- Stress isn't always the non specific result of harm.
- Stress isn't something which must always be avoided.
- Stress is also the spice of life.
- Thus 'stress' means a 'burden', while 'distress' works negatively because of its disharmony and dissonance.
- Stress is the response of the body - and linked with that also the psyche - to all kind of burdens.

 Stress causes (= 'stressors') among others:

Noise	Success-push	Violence	Money problems
Traffic	Haste, speed	Ambition	Frustration
Advertisement	Population	Religious norms	Narrow places
Bad air	Challenges	Working with PC	New technologies
Worry	Driving	Poison	Artificial holiday
Conflict, quarrel	Emission	Wrong authority	Distrust
Sitting	Prestige thinking	Diffuse anxiety	Lying
Lack movement	Wrong nutrition	Moral attitudes	Swindle

What environmental stress but also social stress does to us, can only occur because our physical and psychical adaptability is guided wrongly, wrongly utilized and thus overstrained.

Beside the anxiety for new-learning, also a disability for new-learning and laziness (towards everything that is new) exists; which can be variably strongly conditioned. Also this characteristic depends again indirectly on the phenomenon 'stress'.

Stress works not only by active stimuli (the 'primary stressors') and not only with the biological stress reactions in the organism and their after-effects. Stress also works through the thinking associations which evoke secondary reactions.

 Physical stress reactions are (among others):

🎆 Breathing difficulties	🎆 Migraine	🎆 Urge to pass water
🎆 Stomach pressure	🎆 Irritability	🎆 Sleeping troubles
🎆 Shooting heart pains	🎆 Depression	🎆 Smoking, drinking
🎆 Undue sweating	🎆 Rashes	🎆 Stomach pain
🎆 Nervousness	🎆 Asthma	🎆 Stuttering
🎆 Lack of appetite	🎆 Shaking	🎆 Circulatory disturbance
🎆 Urge to eat and drink	🎆 Shivering	🎆 Gastric ulcer
🎆 Constipation	🎆 Cancer	🎆 Consumption drive
🎆 Diarrhea	🎆 Dizziness	🎆 Diffuse anxiety

→ The effects of stress can last a long time, even when the stressor has stopped its activity.

→ Stress, as an emotional-vegetative reaction of overstraining, arises also through an un-cleared biography, which is activated daily through external stimuli.

Behavior to Prevent and Relieve Stress

'Healthy' dispositions are:

1. Mostly I am aware what sensual feelings I have
2. I can stand up for my opinions and interests
3. I can speak about anger, rage and temper
4. I can accept strong and also unsettled feelings
5. I like new and uncommon ideas
6. I can 'do nothing' without losing the floor under my feet
7. Sometimes I like being alone and I can occupy myself
8. I can spoil myself now and then
9. I don't feel forced to always solve each problem immediately
10. I can live well if things don't go well
11. I walk occasionally (instead of taking the lift or going shopping by car etc.)
12. I often like going out into the fresh air
13. I regularly air my rooms
14. I consciously avoid noise and bad air, if it's possible
15. I don't always need background music
16. I switch off the television if the program bores me
17. I take care to have a regular life pattern
18. I am moderate in smoking, alcohol, coffee, sweets, eating in general
19. I enjoy eating with time and calmness
20. I often enjoy my work
21. I can manage time pressure without 'swerving'
22. I see sense in my work as well as in my leisure
23. I am content with my life situation, I feel good and comfortable
24. I like the environment around my living place
25. I handle electricity, petrol, detergent, medicine, etc. with reason
26. I experience and treat waste ecologically
27. When driving I respect others, and I drive sensibly
28. I take interest in biographies of others in my leisure environment
29. I often visit cultural, social and political events
30. If necessary I forcefully put my interests across
31. My life has sense and value
32. The basic values of human beings are very important for me
33. I can accept suffering in life
34. I don't think that I missed important things/events in my life
35. Today I can accept difficult life phases from my past
36. I am confident of how I create and master my life

Basic theses:

1) Stress as a reaction to overstrain is a complex phenomenon which we have to consider and to judge in the frame of a holistic image of being human.

2) A healthy behavior, as prevention and mastering of stress, has to be developed and practiced also in a holistic understanding of human beings.

3) A healthy behavior is indeed simply a healthy life practice considering the permanent and largely applied education of human beings.

4) We should give the individual life style a life-philosophical foundation with values and attitudes which accept life in its biological and psychical-spiritual entirety.

Notes and Perspectives

What purpose does a conscious reflection about stress factors serve?

Write down the central keywords from this sub-chapter:

What is the human being who is exposed to stress factors for long periods of time?

Explain: 'Healthy dispositions' are important because...:

What did people learn about stress and stress reactions in their parent's home, at school and in the church?

What importance does 'healthy dispositions' have in the communication between life partners?

How do politics and the economy promote the 'healthy dispositions'?

What does advertising convey to us about a lifestyle for health and wellness?

Formulate an important question about reduction of stress:

8.3. Mental Fitness

'Mental' includes: thinking, thoughts, spirit and certainly everything that happens in the mind. 'Being mentally fit' sets the core idea, that the thinking is fresh and capable in its form.

To be in a good state physically is all very well, but it is also important to train the human capacity. To that we count watchfulness, concentration and perception. It is meaningful to educate these mental forces.

If thinking is indolent, the memory weak and thoughtful learning tenacious and the perceptions diffuse, and then this will have negative consequences with increasing age.

If mental forces are well trained, the human being can master his daily affairs more efficiently and the challenges of life too. He sees given things as they are, can analyze them more objectively and recognize reasonable solutions more clearly.

Imagination is also part of the mind. That includes daydreaming, fantasy, intuition and in general the images which we have floating in our consciousness. If man can't meaningfully form these inner realities, then he is oppressed by them and limited in his creative possibilities.

Everybody makes his own positive and negative images about himself and his life. We always unite life experiences with emotionally judged images. Here we can also train mentally.

Examples are: positive imagination, mental psycho-hygiene and 'autogenous' training at an advanced level. With inner ideas we influence our well-being, our behavior and our attitudes about life. This has effects on our daily life, our self-experience, our relationships and our leisure activity.

Well-being is always based on inner images. If we don't keep order there and if our ideas are not thematically elaborated, then chaos dominates the feelings and the interpretation of all experiences. Who wants that? Anybody?

Being mentally fit means that the brain-functions work well. The right hemisphere contains the emotional images. Here you find artistic, spiritual and intuitive forces. The left hemisphere works logically, analytically, and rationally. This part of the brain also processes language.

We can train mental fitness on both parts. We keep thinking fit by: reading, analyzing, memory exercises (e.g. remembering names), clearly defining goals, self-control, making daily plans, etc.

Imaginative abilities that we train, for example, with: contemplating pictures (museums), listening to music, expressing feelings, considering intuitive impulses and of course with methodically handled imagination (for psycho-hygiene, to work out experiences) and through dealing with dreams.

Mental training is much more than 'positive thinking' and 'positive imagination'. The singular forces are trained in their capacity and are kept fresh to master life, to treat efficiently problems and to work out new creations. This is positive and constructive!

Reflections and Discussion

■ Being mentally-fit means 'cognitively':

▪ Clear perception	▪ Objective order	▪ Right sequences
▪ Differentiated words	▪ Logical thinking	▪ Good time-organization
▪ Precise thinking	▪ Detailed facts	▪ High concentration
▪ Reflected aims	▪ Reasonable planning	▪ Fresh memory

■ Being mentally-fit 'emotional-imaginative':

▪ Interest in images	▪ To create inner images	▪ Feeling for balance
▪ Remember dreams	▪ To experience beauty	▪ Wholeness experience
▪ Sensitivity for colors	▪ Imagine experiences	▪ Interest in creations
▪ To experience forms	▪ Clear body experience	▪ Having a keen eye
▪ Spontaneous inspiration	▪ Good time-experience	▪ To convert intuitions

■ Mental fitness can be trained. Classical exercises are:

• Crossword puzzle	• Combine geometrically	• Train point-concentration
• Number-exercises	• Memorize things	• Putting together elements

■ Mental fitness can be trained in life. Our suggestions are:

- Write down what you said and what the other person said after a call
- Go through the previous day and experience the situations again
- Preview the day and plan the coming day imaginatively and by thinking
- Decorate your living room consciously with pictures, change them sometimes
- Leisure activity with pictures, colors, forms, music, movements, nature experience
- Work through difficult situations thoroughly and write down the elements
- Keep a diary about experiences, about others and all kinds of subjects
- Write down your dreams, work through them, draw diagrams, and play with scenarios
- Communicate feelings; express them physically and with constructive actions
- Handle and plan creatively: visits, festivities, presents, being together

■ Mental training happens through confrontation with life:

- Elaborate conflicts precisely and guide them to competent solutions
- Formulate your own values precisely, revise them if necessary
- See through masks and facades; find a clear view for depth
- See everything in a complex network and don't naively simplify things
- Steadily learn new things through systematically aimed reading
- Consciously deal with your life-time and your forces

Diagram 1.24: Concept 'Mental Fitness'

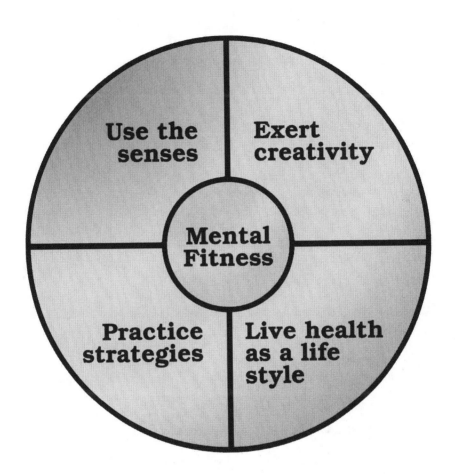

Ways of Systematically Dealing with Problems

If one doesn't want to master problems and difficulties without a plan, or simply by accident, then a strategy is necessary, that means a systematic, open and transparent planning of possible solutions. Few people do this in their everyday life. The effects are evident: bad solutions, no solutions at all, trials without success and a tormenting in endless problems.

Six strategic steps to solve problems:

<u>1st step: Precisely analyzing and organizing the problem</u>
- How is the problem? How did it come about? How important is the problem?
- What is part of the problem? Which institution is involved?
- What is my ideal? Which possibilities are given?

<u>2nd step: Identifying deficit of information, life-knowledge, theories, ideas</u>
- What is the lack of facts, knowledge, theories and ideas?
- Which connections do I not understand?
- Structure ideas and facts, then define the problem in a new way.

<u>3rd step: Constructing theories and procuring the necessary material (information)</u>
- Search for connections and explanations (causes-effects; networking).
- Construct a diagram (draw, course-diagram, mind-mapping, etc.
- Managing a problem is always also a learning process for all people involved.

<u>4th step: Draft of possible solution on the basic of theories (X is because of Y)</u>
- Examine if a solution is feasible. Define the standards of the solution.
- Prepare the decisions. Analyze the concomitant phenomenon and effects.

<u>5th step: Realizing the plan of solution</u>
- Action!

<u>6th step: Evaluation, that means examination of the success</u>
- If necessary, make corrections and try again in a new way.

Everybody has his individual capacity to solve problems, his specific hindering factors and his special abilities. Creativity is decisive. Motivation is essential. Mental fitness is a precondition.

The central question is: "Do you want to solve the problem, or do you prefer to live with it for the next few years, until one day it disappears - or even until it increases enormously?"

Resolving problems always demands: concentration, effort with energy and resources, competent use of time and skills for mastering life, acquiring knowledge, and learning processes.

Sometimes we must learn to efficiently live with problems. Many problems can't be eliminated just like that. To correctly live with problems is also a matter of attitudes.

How to Create 'mentally fit' Leisure

For many people the time after work and the time on weekends are 'problem-times'. They don't have anything meaningful to do and can't do anything with themselves. They suffer from boredom, emptiness and inner isolation. Leisure becomes a depressing 'waste of time'. Some kinds of amusement just help to distract from insufficiency. Most people don't think that they spend their leisure with their biography in the background, with their inner life and with their relationship problems. We put together some ideas which may contribute to a successful leisure. Motto: Be fit in leisure too!

☑ It is recommended, if one takes the time to form an overall concept for the leisure time. This is a basis to define a concrete aim. The more information is collected, the clearer the ideas become about means and ways. Planning works efficiently, when it is realistic. These are the basics for decisions about time-planning and actions. The realization should be evaluated once or twice a year. So it is possible to relate to the overall concept and revise it if necessary.

☑ An organized daily rhythm during the weekend, on free days and on holiday allows a fulfilled leisure. The body reacts with disturbances if the rhythm of movement and calm can't be regulated. Cultivate sensuality with a reasonable nutrition, enough movement and suitable clothes are part of a healthy (prototypical) life style. Freedom doesn't mean being lazy, letting oneself go or 'consumption'. Leisure is a realization of individual possibilities.

☑ Leisure is a chance to talk about current tensions and problems with your life partner, to clear and solve them. In this way we can avoid inner conflicts with the partner piling up and then exploding suddenly and unexpectedly. We can 'ritualize' discussions in partnerships like: time, frame and subjects.

☑ Regularly taking time for oneself and managing inner life isn't only important for oneself. It is favorable for personal relationships and in general for a positive orientation towards the future. Being mentally-fit includes being open for the psychical life of others and seeing how others manage themselves. This way we can avoid conflicts.

☑ We can also keep mentally-fit on holiday: write down dreams daily, relax methodically, meditate systematically, keep a diary, elaborate step by step the past year, read something constructive. Daily overeating and drinking in order to be lazy, roasting in the sun and hanging around bars night after night has nothing to do with relaxation and edification. Self-management is zero here! Holidays which don't contribute to self-education are lost life-time.

☑ 'Learning during the whole life' isn't meant as professional, but can be interpreted as a kind of living. Language knowledge for example is useful in the 'house of Europe'. This can be connected with general (further) education: to get to know other countries and traditions widens the horizon. So we experience and increasingly understand the variety of human beings (psychical, social, political, and religious) under different cultural frame conditions.

☑ Many people experience visiting friends, acquaintances and relatives as stress. Too much chattering there! He who is mentally-fit can bring his life knowledge into play. This may become a benefit for all.

☑ Dealing with feelings must be cultivated if the feelings about life will gain depth. Only in that way can well-feeling become a source of life force. There are many small occasions to care for the beauty of forms (creations).

Notes and Perspectives

How does the (general) daily life of people with mental fitness look like?

Write down the central keywords from this sub-chapter:

What is the human being without mental fitness?

Explain: Mental fitness is important because...:

What did people learn about mental fitness in their parent's home, at school and in the church?

What importance does the systematic elaboration of problems have in the communication between life partners and in the interactions in general?

In what can we see a lack of mental fitness by the people in politics and the economy?

What does advertising impart to us about the skills to master problems?

Formulate an important question about mental fitness:

8.4. Exercises

1. What are your attitudes towards mental fitness?

2. What do you think about caring for a personal lifestyle?

3. What especially worries you about the concept of a 'holistic health'?

4. Healthy dispositions are:

Give heed to the list (in chapter 8.2.), page 'Behavior to prevent and relieve stress', and elaborate in the following way:

4.1. Which are the people's strengths, their healthy dispositions?

4.2. Which are the people's weaknesses?

4.3. What are the consequences from 4.2. for the people's working (professional life)?

4.4. What are the consequences from 4.2. for the people's personal life quality?

4.5. What are you concluding from 4.2., 4.3. and 4.4. for the people's development and Individuation?

5. Stress Factors

5.1. Look back a month with the question: What are your stress factors?

5.2. Which stress factors can you reduce with what kind of measures?

6. Mental fitness. Mark: 4 = total/very   3 = preponderant   2 = middling
1 = moderate

6.a) A majority of people are mentally fit ('cognitive'):

... clear perception
... differentiated use of word
... precise thinking
... analyzed aims
... objective order
... logic thinking
... precise facts
... reasonable planning
... the right succession
... good time organization
... high concentration
... a fresh memory

Total points: …..

6.b) A majority of people are mentally fit ('emotional-imaginative'):

... interest in images
... remembering dreams
... sensation of colors
... experience of form
... spontaneous associations
... creating inner images
... experience of beauty
... imaginary of experiences
... clear body sensation
... good time feeling
... feeling for balance
... sensation of holiness
... interest in creating

... ability for observation in life
... practice intuition

6.c) Mental fitness in life:

... After phoning I remember exactly what we have spoken about
... In my imagination I can go through the past day in my memory without
   difficulties
... I can easily get through past situations with all my feelings
... I can preview a day in my imagination
... I can plan a day with thinking and imagination
... I decorate my living area and I change it sometimes
... I care about images, colors, forms, music, movements, and nature
   experiences
... I can elaborate difficult situations in my thoughts
... I keep a diary about events, other people and all kind of subjects
... I note down my dreams and interpret them
... I can communicate emotions and express them with constructive acts
... I am planning and realizing visits and being together with others
   consciously

6.d) Mental-Training happens also when one confronts oneself with life.
React with an spontaneous statement:

▪ Elaborate thoroughly difficulties and go forward to competent solutions
▪ Formulate own values (attitudes) precisely and, in case, revise them
▪ To see through critically the masks and façades, clear until the deepness
▪ To see everything in the complex network and not simplify naively
▪ Always learning something new by reading systematically and well-aimed

· To deal well and consciously with your own life time and forces

Multiple Choice Test

Choose the four correct answers and mark them with a cross: ☒ a) lust

8.1. What promotes a holistic health?

☐ a) Reduction of conflicts
☐ b) Lustful care for the body
☐ c) Meditation
☐ d) Parties
☐ e) Open minded attitudes
☐ f) The right car type

8.2. Part of a 'holistic health' are:

☐ a) Completely cut out of luxury
☐ b) Experiences of meaning
☐ c) Moral integrity
☐ d) Iron body
☐ e) Freedom from biographical burden
☐ f) Tolerance of frustration

8.3. The concept of mental fitness allows statements like:

☐ a) Mental fitness is preponderantly meant for professional success.
☐ b) Mental fitness guides us to a life free of conflicts and problems.
☐ c) He who doesn't make use of dreams, meditation and intuition, can only be
    restrictedly mentally fit in small limits.
☐ d) He who is mentally fit has a differentiated experience of colors, forms,
    wholeness, time and feelings.
☐ e) Mental fitness contains a high creative potential for leisure activities
    and relationships.
☐ f) Mental fitness adds a specific relaxation, revitalization,
    enrichment and satisfaction to holidays.

9. Partnership between Man and Woman

The relationship between man and woman is a kind of being with high values and a unique possibility of living the personal individuation.

Essential Theses

❑ Self-realization through relationship is a particular challenge, then the patterns from childhood are repeated automatically by each adult:

- Parents: communication, language
- imitating pattern of behavior
- deficit from childhood
- bonds to familial values
- parental punishment
- catch up on unfulfilled puberty
- revive bonds with the parents
- formed bodily experience

❑ In a partnership-like relationship many forces act mutually, for example:

- psycho-dynamism
- dynamism of feelings
- denying lust
- biography
- ability to communicate
- capacity of assimilating
- kind of thinking
- indifference
- fear of bonds/separation
- beliefs
- education (training)
- creativity

❑ Two partners influence each other enormously in the development of personality. The unconscious interplay is decisive for the superficially created living together.

❑ Masculinity and femininity are products of continuous processes of development, which are decisively influenced/transmitted socially. There are many ways of living masculinity and femininity.

❑ If Spirit is masculine and life feminine, then men and women always have both aspects within them. The different forms of experience and expression allow both partners to build up their identity as man and woman through relationship.

❑ This process characterizes basically what a marriage is. Without saying 'yes' to life and to the body and also to the development of love capacity the process in not thoroughly realizable.

9.1. Self-being through a Relationship

The expectations of a relationship are enormous. The sufferings and difficulties in many relationships speak volumes. Human beings wish for harmony, love, happiness, tenderness, joy, fulfillment and peace through being together.

Longing for love, for being in love, eroticism and lust experiences cause a quantity of illusions and hopes which nearly all crumble away during the years.

Many 'stable' relationships fail. It may be better not to judge this. Mainly it isn't adequate to speak about 'guilt'. If we take 'failure' as a critical category, then everywhere people are failing with mostly worse consequences. One can also fail in a 'single'-life. This happens as often!

If we reduce the intensity of well-being feelings, maybe longing or maybe intimate experiences, then we have two people who feel a deep mutual sympathy and estimation. Both have a complex psychical life. Both have a biography with nearly infinite conditioned images and experiences.

The life history of both contains a lot of disordered, unelaborated and connected elements. Both live in a social system - family, acquaintances, and friends, colleagues - in a specific cultural environment and in a working world. Both have their habits, their behavior patterns, their talents, their antipathies towards things, human beings and attitudes. Both have an individual body-relation, an individual lust-experience, habits of eating and clothing, habits of movement, a kind of care for the body and a relation to nature and animals.

A huge amount of beliefs, attitudes and little values stay combined or in contradiction. Also feelings, psycho-dynamism and biorhythm are different. And finally there is also an indissoluble genuine difference between man and woman.

Disappointments, collusions, neurotic development, quarrels, conflicts and even psycho-somatic reactions are preconditioned. Many people try to protect their 'bastion' with religious attitudes or with clever self-deception.

There are many 'arrangements' which sometimes appear as the only solution. The answer for conflicts in relationship isn't psychotherapy! Except if one is indeed psychically ill.

We can only see what we know or that which we are attentive to; for example: the unconscious effects of the biography, the variety of the psychical needs, the ability of the force of love.

He who doesn't take his psychical forces seriously, neither forms his self-management with a clear view nor trains mental fitness, cannot see these realities in his life partner. And he cannot offer a constructive communication and solutions for these subjects.

→ Relationship has to be linked with self-realization, if it is to have a chance.

→ Education is necessary: Self-knowledge, human-knowledge, personality-education.

Reflections and Discussion

■ With a relationship between man and woman many hopes are connected:

▪ peace	▪ tenderness	▪ fidelity	▪ home
▪ happiness	▪ love	▪ coziness	▪ intimacy
▪ joy	▪ being glad	▪ being together	▪ enjoyment
▪ harmony	▪ being cared for	▪ division of work	▪ being for each other
▪ lust-experience	▪ discussions	▪ activities	▪ being united

■ The reality of relationships demonstrates preponderantly another image:

▪ divorce	▪ infidelity	▪ aggression	▪ power-play
▪ quarrels	▪ tensions	▪ boredom	▪ anxiety
▪ violence	▪ sexual problems	▪ lies, dishonesty	▪ depressions
▪ disappointments	▪ regressions	▪ being silent	▪ dominance

• divorce	• eruptions	• suppressing	• sadism

■ In each relationship without psychical education, sooner or later the repetitions of the individual experiences from the childhood come up:

- imitating mother (as woman)
- imitating father (as man)
- repeating parental patterns of quarrelling
- parental punishing
- effects of super-ego, formed in childhood
- linked to familial patterns of value
- repetition of typical daily patterns
- imitating the language of the parents
- reactivation of early relation to the parents
- make up for earlier trials to break free
- trying to satisfy deficits from childhood
- make up for the unfinished puberty
- anxiety about being separated from parents
- style of parental talk at the table
- patterns of conflict concerning house work
- flight to mother/father (as protection)

■ Self-realization through personality education and individuation is a precondition for a successful relationship. A partnership-relation (married life) is a kind of living, with mutual understanding and participation with the aim to realize this human being together. Having and educating children, the creation of a new family life can be a chance to reflect individual experiences, to work them out and to live new forms with self-education:

- to integrate the partner into one's self-education (communication, participation)
- to realize oneself and to do everything so that the partner can also realize himself
- to form one's own masculinity (femininity) in the psyche through the partner
- to increase the force of love to find out together the 'mystery of life'

Diagram 1.25: Dimensions of a Partnership-like Living

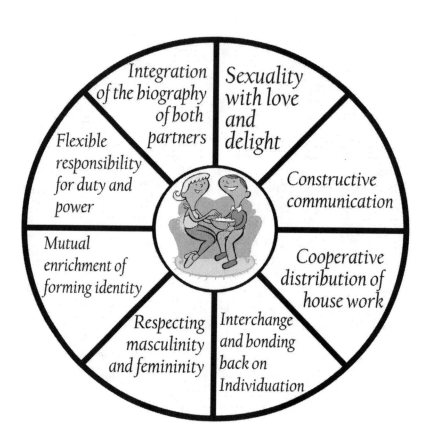

Integration of the biography of both partners

Sexuality with love and delight

Flexible responsibility for duty and power

Constructive communication

Mutual enrichment of forming identity

Cooperative distribution of house work

Respecting masculinity and femininity

Interchange and bonding back on Individuation

The Difficulties in a Love Relationship

Incidents in the life course of both partners play an important impact in the relationship, even if these incidents date back many years; und it is like that until these incidents are worked out:

▪ Traumatic events	▪ Failures in school	▪ Earlier failed relationships
▪ Divorce of the parents	▪ Sexual disillusionment	▪ Absence of father / mother
▪ Rejected from the parent	▪ Professional failure	▪ Addiction father / mother
▪ Lack of love in the childhood	▪ Religious education	▪ Ideological father / mother
▪ Disease in the parent's family	▪ Religious education	▪ Interruption of pregnancy
▪ Poverty / wealth (parents)	▪ Good parent's relationship	▪ Psychical disorder (parents)
▪ Punishing style of the parents	▪ Conflictive childhood	

Varied situations arise in the daily life of a relationship, giving cause for quarrel:

- Not clearly and concretely expressing one's own needs, also for leisure
- Misunderstandings (e.g. expected behavior) because of unclear communication
- Ignoring something with the purpose of avoiding arguments
- Not giving importance to one's own feelings and to the one's of the partner
- Preoccupied excessively with oneself, instead of being concentrated in the present
- To be stressed meanwhile giving low attention to the partner
- Starting an important communication at an inappropriate time and timeframe
- Not early enough planning and taking decisions about what is important and urgent
- Eating and drinking, also watching TV, because of being frustrated and bored
- To please the partner in a way one basically doesn't want to
- Not admitting to be deeply preoccupied with oneself
- To behave aggressively to create distance or to suppress something

- To behave affectedly, to play the offended and annoyed person
- Not being punctual as a hidden way of manipulating the partner
- Making a mess as a form of a strike or protest in relationship matters
- Being unsatisfied as a result of a deficit of common life aims
- Problems with money and disagreements about dealing with money (consumption)
- All life lies create arguments as soon as the partner refuses them

To find new views and attitudes:

☺ Talking to each other is a learning process; e.g. contemplating about talking.

☺ Each partnership has sometimes strong arguments.

☺ Some quarrels may cover deeper emotions; e.g. about love and trust.

☺ To have a strong confrontation with the partner is sometimes necessary.

☺ With the duration of a relationship differences may grow too.

☺ Arguments about banalities are normal; e.g. order, home work, cooking, etc.

☺ Total harmony doesn't exist; this is a life lie.

☺ If one creates a baby, one must know: Sex life will change from that day on.

☺ A humiliating criticism at the working place is often affecting the life at home.

☺ Frustration at work converts sometimes rapidly into a frustration in the relationship.

☺ Good friends can sometimes produce even more problems in a difficult situation.

☺ Dogmas and ideologies are poison for a partnership with Individuation.

☺ Sometimes one has to contemplate: "Do I really want to destroy my relationship?"

Resolving conflicts in a relationship demands ability to love, also acknowledge that the destiny of a relationship depends on how the partners deal with polarities: the space they want to give for experiencing, passive enjoyments and activities; mutual interplay with a more active and passive role; the limits they give to exploring and acting or suppressing, etc.

Characteristics of Partnership

Partnership is an ideal of a modern relationship between man and woman.

We formulate some theses from an overview of actual books on that subject:

- Partnership is not equal relationship, but contains specific characteristics.
- Mutual interest for daily reality is essential for both partners.
- Openness for the real life of both partners always also contains conflicts.
- Partners respect each other in their different being (character, gender).
- Reciprocity (reversibility) and thus equal standing are considered to be principles.
- Closeness and distance periodically, form a normal part of being together.
- The biography of each is as important as the respective identities.
- Love promotes individuation, and thus the individual human creation.
- Partners communicate about their differences and things they have in common.
- Partnership is not a static state according to a contract, but a process.
- Partners respect the limitations of each other and the 'world' of the other.
- Partners know that limits can't be crossed at any time.
- Daily life takes up a central space, has to be organized by talking about it.
- Love in the partnership must be regularly stimulated and formed.
- Partnership regulates the common things by communication.
- The power-situation is balanced, and has to be worked at, daily.
- In the partnership the mistakes of both are not calculated.
- Self-realization (forming of the identity) implies self-devotion.
- Reason and intelligence are basic functions, but they don't guarantee love.
- Eroticism and being in love have their place in the normality of daily life.
- To live in a partnership is strenuous and demands a qualified self-management.
- Moments of symbiotic feelings may have a place in the normality of the daily life.
- Partnership-like love isn't possible without tensions and risks.
- The partners don't 'possess' each other with their whole being.
- Seduction and lust are forces equally dynamic as objectivity.
- The mutual dependence of sexual satisfaction is not against autonomy.
- The ability to understand belongs to the ability for love; this is strenuous.
- Partners can deal with the 'inner child' of each other.
- The parallel development of identity stands in a reciprocal dynamism.
- Both partners know: every few years the self-identity changes.
- In a partnership ego-feelings and sexual experiences are encouraged.
- Partners mutually create their femininity and masculinity.

- Also by solving objective questions both are a 'team'.
- Working out the unconscious life (the biography) is partly a shared activity.
- Partners orientate commonly on their dreams, intuitions and meditations.
- Partners enrich each other mutually with creative actions during their leisure.
- In a partnership a role division can be accepted.

Notes and Perspectives

What purpose does partnership serve in relationships?

Write down the central keywords from this sub-chapter:

What is the human being in human relation to others without partnership?

Explain: Partnership rules in a relationship are important because…:

What did people learn about partnership in the relationship between man and woman in their parent's home, at school and in the church?

What importance does partnership have in the communication between life partners and in the interactions in general?

How do politics and the economy practice the characteristics of partnership?

What does advertising impart to us about partnership in the relationship between man and woman?

Formulate an important question about living together with partnership:

9.2. Psycho-Dynamics of the Interplay

With the matrimonial bond no magic happens. Each one maintains his character, the characteristics of his personality, his shadows and ideals. Most people have little tics, compulsions, anxieties and 'hysteric' or 'anal' reactions. If 'neurotic disturbance' means that some experiences (bonds or drives) are suppressed, acting periodically in a converted matter, then nearly all people have a 'share' of this.

Probably everybody is a 'defense-player': suppressing, displacing, changing into the opposite, isolating, identifying, projecting, denying etc. 'Character' always means a psycho-dynamism formed in a certain way, as for example: introverted, choleric, compulsive, unending complaining, superficial etc.

Such formed shapes don't disappear with the beginning of living together. Being in love may cover realities, but the 'shadows' break through some time, often as a psycho-somatic illness. Or both are identifying with an ideology or with dogmas which will maintain the 'harmony'.

Both partners bring portions into the common life, mostly complementing each other. All these psychical aspects create in each relationship a decisive dynamism. The one, who knows that, can learn to guide and form these forces. This only functions with love, and with a lot of communication.

Furthermore there are the 'complexes'. These are the unelaborated subjects from the biography. Unconscious bonds with father and mother often have dramatic impacts on a marriage. Embarrassing experiences, over all heavy feelings of guilt, have a long echo in the future.

Sexual difficulties, sad, humiliating experiences, failure and feelings of inferiority undermine sexual experiences and sexual activities in the new being together. Unsettled earlier friendships or an unelaborated divorce can't be swept under the carpet. Complexes decisively form the interplay. Worst 'traps' are: "I love you, even if you don't love me", or "I only love you, when you love me unconditionally". To that comes the secret desire to be always loved, and often anxiety of separation and bonds.

With all that the illusions of harmony and happiness crumble away easily. If the partners don't succeed in freeing these subjects, then they dominate subliminally more and more.

Partners influence each other enormously in the development of personality, in a positive and negative way. Moreover, the process is embedded in an environment: work, parents-in-law, brother and sister, friends, church, advertisements etc. Such external factors contribute to the psycho-dynamism of a relationship.

An evolutionary development of the relationship presupposes a thorough dealing with such life themes. For good success a reduction of external influences might sometimes be a solution.

Reflections and Discussion

■ In a relationship the whole human being is acting, along with the biography back to the earliest childhood. Character and habits can rarely stay concealed for years:

• being introverted/extroverted	• egoism
• desire of power and dominance	• narcissism
• feelings of inferiority	• moods
• anxiety and depression	• laziness and carelessness
• tics and 'small' compulsions	• nagging
• opinions about order	• condemning valuation
• mechanism of suppressing	• denying of lust and desire of lust

■ Many events in the biography of both partners 'play together' in the relationship, even if they date back years, so long until they are elaborated:

• poverty or wealth in parent's home	• failure at school
• divorce of the parents	• absence of father/mother
• being rejected by the parents	• psychical disorder of father/mother
• deficiency of love in the childhood	• sad experiences in the childhood

▪ illnesses in the family	▪ professional failure
▪ sexual disappointments	▪ religious education
▪ earlier failed relationships	▪ ideological 'milieu' in parent's home
▪ addiction in the parent's home	▪ termination of pregnancy
▪ punishing education style of the parents	▪ failure at school

■ The inner system of values of both partners, even if it is subliminal during a long period, with time pushes itself more and more into daily life.

Aspects are: ideological, philosophical and religious ideas. If these values can't be communicated, reflected and revised, severe tensions and conflicts start increasing. We think here of values and attitudes like:

- order in the household
- distribution of work and roles
- sexual experience and behavior
- creating meetings and visits
- fidelity and adultery
- masculine and feminine emancipation
- judging aggression
- adaptability and being creative
- termination of pregnancy
- needs for autonomy and freedom
- religious and spiritual practice
- importance of personality education

■ The more each partner forms himself through individuation including the other in this process, the better a relationship can evolve. From this an optimal dynamism for a fulfilled relationship can grow.

Diagram 1.26: The Psychical-Spiritual and Social Interplay

Feelings
Needs
Consciousness
Psycho-dynamism
Love
Unconscious
Spirit
Intelligence
Ego-forces

Feelings
Needs
Consciousness
Psycho-dynamism
Love
Unconscious
Spirit
Intelligence
Ego-forces

Dealing with Quarrels and Conflicts

There are a lot of starting possibilities, how to deal in a relationship with quarrels and conflicts. Suggestions:

- Each one practices, continuously and thoroughly on his own way, self-knowledge and Individuation.
- Each one regularly makes efforts understanding oneself and the partner.
- Each one deals seriously with his own dreams. Both promote these efforts. Thereby, the power who creates the dreams – the inner spirit – knows perfectly how to guide each one (with dreams) aiming a constructive growing of the relationship.
- Both accept and integrate the complexity of the psychical life. This presupposes that both acquire knowledge, e.g. through courses.
- Each one explores the other regularly, explain oneself clearly and accept the partner as a human being in a permanent evolutionary process of growth.
- Both promote the partner mutually in the all-sided development of being a man / a woman, considering the inner images about the other gender, named „anima" and „animus" which have to be formed too.
- Through dialogue exploring and forming the basic values, clarify the attitudes and beliefs, working out in common a revision.
- Both understand self-management as a matter of partnership, forming roles for the daily living together: order, punctuality, home work, responsibilities, moments for serious discussions and relaxation, lists for shopping, ideas for leisure and holidays, etc.
- Both create the homely atmosphere to feel well and a place for each one for reading, books, writing, administrations, etc.
- Each one forms his self-identity with a strong focus on the partner (the other gender), being aware of this reality, talking about and differentiating it.
- Both have some contacts in leisure; have a hobby or a cultural (social) activity. But this life area shouldn't be an area of replacement for an unsatisfied relationship.
- Both create regularly common experiences to enjoy life. Part of that are moments of common relaxation and of a non verbal being together in the sense of: "It is beautiful, that you are here in my life!"
- Both talk about everything concerning life, also about petty matters. Acting in the interest of both has to be transparent, prepared and discussed (before / after). Both promote the other in his life skills.
- Each one talks about his personal biography and the common history of their relationship; both try to understand and to elaborate these

experiences. The common history of relationship and the common plans for the future also form a sort of partner-identity.

- Both respect that each one stays for ever in his own being and development as an individual; and that they can never become a symbiosis. Both partner knows, respects and promotes the attitude that each one has to learn a lot during the whole life about psychical life, love, emotions and sex.
- Both stimulate regularly creative activities in all life areas, also in the sexual life. Both can talk about without feeling ridicule and being shamed.
- Both learn how to argue without controlling each other with life lies and defense games. Both consider the communication roles and the strategies for problem solving.
- Both do not balance mutually their errors. Both learn to forgive and to reconcile, also after a heavy fight. The ability to love with its development and reinforcement is demanding this.
- Both reduce one's own life lies without reproach and give higher importance to the psychical life as to the external values. Thus, what is the partner in the relationship without his psychical life?

Constructive Communication in the Partnership

Diverse scientific books explore some conditions and rules which are important for a constructive mastering of life:

a) 15 rules for a partnership-like communication:

1. Don't humiliate, don't hurt, don't depreciate, and don't sneer about the partner
2. Don't horn in, don't exaggerate, don't play down, don't lose the 'tone'
3. Talk together about matters cooperatively, mutually, complementary
4. Speak definitely, clearly, objectively, distinguished, open and direct
5. Listening, understanding, giving importance, selecting, letting the other speak
6. To allow problems, wishes, questions and over all feelings
7. To keep and allow limitation and autonomy
8. Respect the partner as an independent person, keeping the own limitation
9. Pay attention to spiritual rootedness (dreams), to intuition and inner resonance
10. Responsibility for place, room, time, course, duration, aim, choice, termination
11. Keep away from external influences (television, other people)
12. Consider one's own physical state and also the other's

13. Being persevering but still flexible; keep an eye on the course of communication
14. Understand passed things as a challenge to work them out, not as reproaches
15. Periodically reflect upon values, norms and attitudes; revise them if necessary

b) Some theses which could help to improve communication:

- In a discussion there are more realities given than one may think.
- Complete consensus is rarely possible.
- Misunderstanding is normal.
- Conflicts and arguments are part of life.
- To talk about talking improves the understanding.
- One can't talk better than one perceives and thinks.
- Speaking is also always an expression of previous thinking and feeling.
- To talk is a very important way of mastering realities
- Communication is always more related to human beings than to things.
- To infringe sometimes upon the rules of a good communication is human.

c) Human aspects in talks (discussions):

□projections	□inner pressure	□self-confidence
□perception	□individual language (code)	□feeling of inferiority
□prejudices	□fear of punishment	□power desire
□need for protection	□roles in the situation	□defense mechanism
□feelings of guilt	□covered interests	□the appearance of a person
□anxiety of life	□ego-orientation	□inhibitions

d) A good communication support at long time:

☐ readiness for learning	☐ autonomy	☐ forming new values
☐ development, growth	☐ responsibility	☐ new forms of living
☐ love	☐ peace	☐ transparency
☐ clearing and solutions	☐ more knowledge	☐ respect
☐ cooperation	☐ de-mythologizing	☐ reciprocity
☐ fairness	☐ being together	☐ openness
☐ adaptation	☐ motivation	☐ learning processes
☐ trust	☐ wholeness	☐ initiative
☐ respect	☐ understanding	☐ truthfulness

Notes and Perspectives

What purpose does constructive communication serve in daily life?

Write down the central keywords from this sub-chapter:

What is the human being in relationships without mutual integration of the psychical organism?

Explain: Ability to love is important because…:

What did people learn about constructive and partnership-like communication in their parent's home, at school and in the church?

What importance the '15 rules for a constructive communication' have in the communication between life partners and in the interactions in general?

How do politics and the economy handle the constructive communication?

What does advertising impart to us about ability of loving?

Formulate an important question about constructive communication:

9.3. Re-discovery of Being a Woman / Being a Man

A man and a woman living together, decided as a common course for life, is one of the most valuable kinds of living. The institution 'marriage' is created culturally for that. This isn't the same as a homosexual or a lesbian partnership.

Man and woman differ not only biologically (sexual) and through educational influences. The psychic life as a wholeness 'functions' differently. Masculine and feminine roles are not merely a product of learning processes.

Masculinity and femininity exist as a quality. That is linked psychically and physically, although in many ways deformable and in mutual action. Many marriages fail and are really 'ill' because they are thoroughly destructive and function with masks (lies). This fact doesn't speak against the high value of the institution 'marriage', of man and woman living together. Here is a great lack of self-education.

That a man has to know: a man isn't a woman! And a woman should have in her eye: he is a man! It is a life challenge to search that, to discover and to integrate this into the psychical-spiritual life; and this not only as a matter of sexual difference! The matriarchal and patriarchal symbols are to be overcome. We have to find the truthful covered archetypes.

The genuine feminine image is the creative principle of life, the donator and preserver of life. The divine mother and the love-divinity are highest representations of femininity. Men are socialized for violence, strength, destruction, indigence of feelings, as the conqueror, maker etc.

What could be his genuine image? He also can (paternally) be as caring as a woman can think rationally. He also should have feelings like a woman. Without speaking in clichés, procreating of life, of 'projects' and managing these is an aspect of masculinity.

Perhaps it is like that: Spirit is masculine and life is a genuine feminine force (of life). Certainly man and woman have both these forces inside. Masculine and feminine forces are different, but not in their value. Both can live only with and through the other.

All actions, in private life as in social life and in the spirituality, can occur in partnership-like interests and tendency. Also a woman can be a priest, a general director or a state president; she doesn't have to become 'male' for that. On the other hand a man can be creative in household work as well in education and in forming daily life, without being 'female.

Essential:

→ Man and woman can bring forward evolutionary terrestrial life only with solidarity and cooperation, if both realize the inner evolution.

→ This applies to matrimonial life as well as political-economical and social life.

Reflections and Discussion

■ About being man and being woman we have different images and opinions in our society, and also in psychology. Women still do not receive their adequate value and place in Europe and worldwide. Classical prejudices are for example:

a) Man: rigid, violent, quarrelsome, pugnacious, authoritarian, imperious, domineering

b) Women: inconsiderate, moody, irrational, sensible, hysterical, and seductive

■ In relationships and in living-together we still often find a division of labor after the traditional pattern:

a) Man: working, procuring money, 'steering', organizing, punishing, 'master' in the home:

b) Woman: household work, cleaning, washing clothes, cooking, children, looking after children's homework:

■ It may be about time to change certain prejudices (images) about femininity and masculinity through new constructive images; to revise are for example:

a) Man: the thinker, the strong, the one who takes initiatives, the violent one only wants sex:

b) Woman: The lovely caring mother, the saintly woman, the prostitute, the attractive woman:

■ Man and woman are not two polar existences; they each realize a part which becomes a completely new wholeness through the other part.

Marriage is a possibility for creating this wholeness. Thus it has a very high value as a form of life both individually and socially. But most of these complementing aspects can be realized in all sections of our social life. This aims at a new form of living.

From a philosophical and transcendental point of view: Life becomes realization of life in the unity of masculinity and femininity.

■ In the daily life of a relationship we see much mutual enrichment; differences we can find in the sections:

- Associations about subjects of life
- Giving importance to logic
- Experiencing important existential situations
- Holistic empathy
- Principles and claims about life
- Helping those in need of care
- Creating an emotional environment
- Checking daily courses
- Behavior of providing
- Physical hard work
- Protecting indigent life
- Taking care of sensitivity
- Creative dealing with meetings
- Holistic experience of the other

Diagram 1.27: Creating Masculinity and Femininity

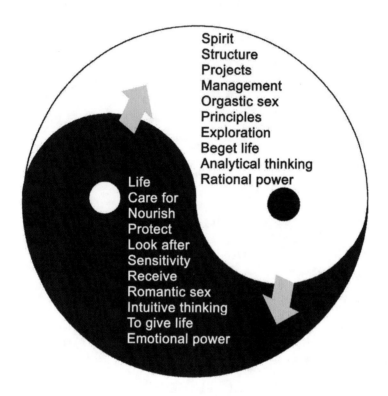

Spirit
Structure
Projects
Management
Orgastic sex
Principles
Exploration
Beget life
Analytical thinking
Rational power

Life
Care for
Nourish
Protect
Look after
Sensitivity
Receive
Romantic sex
Intuitive thinking
To give life
Emotional power

Thesis for the man:

If a man cannot form his masculine principles in a balance and orientation with feminine principles, so he is a destructive man and not a really developed man.

Thesis for the woman:

If a woman cannot form her feminine principles in a balance and orientation with masculine principles, so she is a destructive woman and not a really developed woman.

Aspects of Man and Woman – Anima and Animus

Each person has deepened images about: being father, mother, child, man, and woman. Life experiences convert into human images in the subconscious. An image contains a huge amount of elements. These elements can be opposite and contrary, positive and negative at the same time. This manifoldness of human images stored in the subconscious automatically form a type, wholeness, prototype about: father, mother, child, woman, teacher, priest, policeman, chief, etc.

The inner fragments of such images are emotional and influence as psychical forces unconsciously the person in his life and growing as a man or a woman. These prototypes also form the inner pole of the opposite psychical gender: Is the person a man, we name this inner pole 'Anima'; is the person a woman, we name this inner pole 'Animus'.

In the center of all prototypes stays a concentrated typical image about the opposite gender, by men it is a woman (Anima) and by women it is a man (Animus). The more the singular basic images from real life experiences are split and are in a contradictory tension, the more the whole complex image is in an inner contradiction.

Anima and Animus in the interplay with the external person:

The more the components of a prototype are unbalanced (about men; about women), and therefore acting against each other, the more the whole image (Anima, Animus) is unbalanced. Its components are expressed in extreme images: the self-sacrificing woman or the prostitute, the undeveloped child and the bitch (as an avenger).

The Anima in its undeveloped state has three components in an opposite tension. The man as a real person tends to live an ideal of man alienating him from himself. At the same time he is partly an undeveloped and denied boy. As the third main component we can identify a suppressed despot. Corresponding to that complexity we can identify the same components (inner masculine pole and real female person) by a woman.

Anima and Animus as determined forces by choosing a partner:

This dynamic of inner image (components of the other gender pole) and external aspects (personality) is acting, when a person is looking for a partner.

One person may be attracted more on components of an ideal; another person may be touched more by the undeveloped part of the other person. Behind the lovely man is the undeveloped boy; and behind the conflict-free woman is a brave (good) child. A scarifying woman fulfills ideals of a mother; and behind a caring man we can identify a suppressed man. In real life the variants are manifold.

The complementary parts of the inner image (type) develop a varied activity. Heavy emotional conflicts arise often together with the "shadows" (aspects of the character of a person).

How to renew Anima and Animus:

A person can form his inner psychical pole of the other gender. The masculine and the feminine inner pole can be transformed into an open, constructive unity for living. The solution starts with self-education: One has first to recognize his own shadows and character traits. Then one has to transform these psychical aspects into constructive and life-oriented components. In the core a person has to form his own self-identity as a man, respectively as a woman. This process is an essential function of a marriage respectively of a long term relationship between a man and a woman.

The Gender Relation in Change

We formulate some facts and theses, based on scientific results of the sexual socialization:

1. To examine gender as a variable of personality, abstracted from the context, appears today unavailing.
2. The masculine body is socialized roughly kinetic and movement-intensive, exploring physical activities (in the terrestrial environment), orientated to perform and function; the feminine body (is socialized) rather finely kinetic and promoting aesthetics and attractiveness.
3. The centre of stereotypes about sex: women are emotional, rather anxious, they feel more quickly sad and helpless than men; men are rational, that means less emotional; they may have problems with aggression.
4. Masculinity and femininity are products of continuous processes of construction. This reality is made; it grows from social acting.
5. The relationship between the sexes is negotiated and embattled. Possibilities for changes are also a question of power and material resources.

6. The work division provides paid employment for men (outside from the home). Women are in charge of private daily work. Still only a few men are ready to participate in the education of children and house work.

7. The hierarchy of sexes: In profession and politics, also in science and culture the higher and more powerful positions are almost exclusively occupied by men.

8. Men have by tendency a present readiness for violence. Opposite to that stands the 'power' of mothers over the children, often emotionally over men.

9. There exists an almost compulsive classification of women about men and their sexual wishes.

10. Masculinity grows in the interplay of power, work division and organization of sexuality.

11. The two-sex-system basically structures our society, interactions and individual psycho-dynamism.

12. The education of boys' identity is a strenuous, limiting process, forced from the outside by the mother; is a process of devaluating and negating femininity, grown through the relation to the mother, and femininity in the world.

13. The girl-identity develops through identification and communication with the mother, staying in relation to her, but with that also more incomplete, oppressing the desire for autonomy.

14. Women, who reach a high level of individual autonomy, develop a balance between autonomy and bonds.

15. The 'normal feminine biography' doesn't exist any more. Women today have more interest in material independency, contacts with colleagues, participation in other life areas, appreciation of their performance etc. Yet the gap between interests and professional changes remains.

16. Never before have the demands on a 'good mother' been so high. Feelings of guilt and failure are pre-programmed.

17. Women widen their options; their conflicts intensify.

18. Forms of living can nowadays be chosen and changed. This creates room for action and for negotiating possibilities for both sexes.

19. The unbalanced power in reality and in the mind influences the chances for negotiating furthermore in favor of men, although women are clearly in the offensive. Women demand other forms of relationships and a different work division.

20. Women and in a smaller amount also men can/must change their 'self-concept' several times and roles in their life. Rigid masculine and feminine identity is much less possible.

21. There are plenty of possibilities for living masculinity and femininity.

Notes and Perspectives

What purpose does forming masculinity and femininity serve concretely in daily life?

Write down the central keywords from this sub-chapter:

What is the human being without forming masculinity and femininity?

Explain: Discovering being-man respectively being-woman is important because…:

What did people learn about being-man and being-woman in their parent's home, at school and in the church?

What importance does 'forming masculinity' and 'forming femininity' have in the communication between life partners and in the interactions in general?

How do politics and the economy demonstrate to us the relationship between the two sexes?

What does advertising impart to us about a) being-man; and b) being-woman?

Formulate an important question about the relationship between the two sexes:

9.4. Exercises

1. What are your attitudes towards married life concerning 'partnership'?

2. What have you not yet experienced about partnership/in your partnership until today?

3. What kind of 'games' in the relationship (power, lies, rejecting) do you deal badly with?

4. Relationship between man and woman is an elemental part of life. Which of the following positive aspects do people experience and live today?

Mark: Rarely experience = 1; Sometimes experience = 2 ;
Often experience = 3

☐ Partnership is something especially valuable.
☐ Mutual interest in the daily reality.
☐ Accepting conflicts and mastering experiences.
☐ Respect for the difference (Character, gender).
☐ Mutuality and equality (of rank).
☐ Alternate nearness and distance in living together.
☐ The biography of both as a part of the self-identity.
☐ Understanding about the differences and mutuality.
☐ Respecting the limits of the partner and his "world".
☐ Daily life as a space of conscious communication.
☐ Permanent animation and formation of love.
☐ Daily discussion of all common questions.
☐ No mutual balance of errors.
☐ Self-realization as a dedication of one self.
☐ Reason and intelligence are basically supporting functions.
☐ Erotic and falling in love have their place in the normality of the daily life.
☐ Both with a high level of self-management.

- ☐ Accepting moments of symbiotic emotions.
- ☐ Accepting tensions and risks.
- ☐ Mutual acceptance and satisfaction of the sexual lust.
- ☐ No mutual demand on possession of the wholeness of being.
- ☐ Seduction and lust as animating forces.
- ☐ Mutual sexual satisfaction without reduction of autonomy.
- ☐ Capacity and effort for understanding.
- ☐ Mutual constructive dealing with the inner child.
- ☐ Experience of transformation of the self-identity in periods of a few years.
- ☐ Mutual support oh the ego-feeling and the sexual experience.
- ☐ Mutual realization of the femininity and masculinity.
- ☐ Common solution in objective questions.
- ☐ Partly common elaboration of the unconscious (the biography).
- ☐ Common orientation on dreams, intuition and meditation.
- ☐ Mutual enrichment with a creative using of the leisure time.
- ☐ Discussed and accepted distribution of roles.

What are your conclusions for changes?

5. This is the way people care about their communication (process, sale, control, care, advise; and the discussion in the family, the relationship, the leisure):

Chose a person/a group of persons: ....
And mark with an 'X':

☐ objective	☐ with constancy	☐ slow-heavy
☐ original	☐ awake ('Kairos')	☐ volatile
☐ honest	☐ concentrated	☐ chaotic
☐ transparent	☐ competent in objectives	☐ restless
☐ conscientious	☐ informative	☐ business like
☐ open	☐ flexible in aims	☐ without inner bond
☐ spontaneous	☐ consciously controlled	☐ tricky

☐ efficient in time	☐ adapting actively	☐ fearful
☐ organized	☐ planned	☐ not engaged
☐ exact	☐ prepared	☐ undecided
☐ profoundly	☐ harmonizing	☐ indifferent
☐ asking questions	☐ simple in tendency	☐ short/concise
☐ mandatory	☐ stimulating	☐ directive/controlling
☐ cautious	☐ adequate timing	☐ without questioning
☐ cooperative	☐ seriously	☐ dishonest
☐ well listening	☐ well ordered	☐ aggressive

How do you value the kind of dealing with interaction in the world of business?

6. How do people treat their partner, friends, acquaintances, the children and adolescents?

Chose a person/a group of persons: ……………………….......
And mark with an 'X':

☐ friendly	☐ fair	☐ dominant
☐ talkative	☐ helpful	☐ ego-centric
☐ appreciating	☐ authentic	☐ directive
☐ polite	☐ waiting	☐ aggressive
☐ adapted on the person	☐ mutual	☐ obliging
☐ adaptable in style/theme	☐ attentive	☐ with inner limitation

☐ serving	☐ reliable	☐ impatient
☐ objectively	☐ cooperative	☐ distance less
☐ with distance	☐ dynamic	☐ emotionally
☐ careful	☐ reinforcing	☐ breaking resistance
☐ flexible in style / theme	☐ diplomatic	☐ loose contact
☐ cheerful		☐ with masks
☐ flexible in style / theme		☐ provocative

Interpret your result:

Multiple Choice Test

Choose the four correct answers and mark them with a cross: ☒ a) lust

9.1. Which are the basic characteristics of a partnership?

☐ a) Stay always the same person for the other
☐ b) A constant harmonious unity
☐ c) A parallel-going development of personality
☐ d) Balanced nearness and distance
☐ e) Share the process of individuation
☐ f) Communication above all

9.2. The concept of 'partnership' allows the following statements:

☐ a) In a partnership always the whole human being is involved with his biography.
☐ b) It is important that both partners read the same newspaper, magazines and books.
☐ c) In a partnership sexual wishes and experiences are communicated.
☐ d) Fidelity and adultery are normal rules in a partnership.
☐ e) Common activities are discussed and planned together.
☐ f) The rules of a constructive communication have to be trained over the years.

9.3. In a tendency, the following characteristics are meaningful livable as specifically masculine (feminine):

☐ a) To give importance to 'logic' in daily life
☐ b) Physical hard (technical) work
☐ c) Creating an emotional environment
☐ d) Dealing with money
☐ e) Dividing house work
☐ f) To sign contracts

10. Love and Sexuality

Living a pleasurable sexuality with love is important and difficult; then it is a psychical-spiritual possibility to discover oneself and your partner to form your self-identity.

Essential Theses

❑ To live sexuality isn't free of values. Then love is more than just a feeling, is essentially value and meaning. Sexuality has in practice very different human qualities.

❑ Acceptance of sexuality is saying 'yes' to the masculine and feminine human being. That is much more than acceptance of sexual lust. Only in that acceptance can the human being entirely elaborate his individuation.

❑ Sexual experiencing and acting have to be learned, if one wants to realize the human being and to experience a deep fulfilled happiness. To that belongs for example:

- to interpret the play of contacts
- increase self-esteem with sexuality
- to elaborate activated memories
- to consider emotional disturbances
- messages of tenderness
- to free the mind from burden
- to guide the lust experience
- open-minded attitudes

❑ We form with sexuality our self-identity, for example:

- Abilities for roles
- Self-reflection
- Ability for pleasure
- Acceptance of instinct nature
- Autonomy
- Self-esteem

❑ Men and women experience the interplay of tenderness differently, the embraces and the orgasm, also if the increasing of lust and the energetic relaxation can be equally defined concerning biological and psycho-energetic (libido) aspects.

❑ Sexuality with love and lust, as a part of Individuation of both partners, includes highest values of the human being. The question is put to everybody: "What do I want to invest in order to reach this?"

10.1. To Love Sexuality

Sexual lust is today certainly more accepted than 20 years ago. Many people can live with intimate tenderness, intercourse and masturbation free of moralizing and attitudes hostile to life. But more: Sex-supermarket and sex-services of all kinds are expanding more than ever. Some offers may be helpful, also for learning. But many of these hinder man and woman to love profoundly sexuality.

In sexual life everything is allowed, some say; others experience sexuality with vulnerability, with most intimate sensibility, with values and limits. Reproduction is one aspect. Self-experience, lust, relaxation and intimate experiences of the partner allow a deep, enriching acceptance of life. Consumption and 'free love' seams to break all limits; a reaction against centuries-old hostile attitude about sexuality!

In earlier times sexuality was burdened with guilt and shame. Lust and joy are today in unlimited expansion. Is that 'bad'? Human beings satisfy themselves with eating, drinking and with sweets, cars, clothes, amusements or a foam bath and much more. A wide sensual experience has become a daily aim.

Bodily experiences and sensuality are a central part of our life.

The main question is not "How much sexual satisfaction alone or with others is still 'healthy' (not-neurotic)?", but rather: "How can the human being live his sexual satisfaction constructively and in a fulfilling way?"

In the sexual experience we are sensitive, intimately touched and vulnerable, either lacking a partner or confronted with a partner. Everybody is required to say 'yes' to himself, to his experience and actions; to integrate his needs in his identity and to create his fulfillment of happiness with delight. That is more than 'sexual relaxation'. This is 'self-discovering', encountering oneself and the other, devotion and self-relation. This can be done mechanistically, creatively and with love.

Without the ability of enjoyment, lust isn't fulfilling happiness. But how could happiness be, if in the sexual life only stimulus with lust and not the human being are at the centre of experience and action?

The fast reaction of a lust-experience under the blanket is not a loving sexual practice; it may be comparable with a hasty bite of a dry, cold hamburger. A tender contact is more than sensing of touch and skin.

Tenderness is a symbolic action. It contains a message to 'you', and it contains the experience of the response. It is similar with all variants of sexual plays. They inform the partner about something and they are an experience of the effects, bodily, psychically and spiritually.

→ To love sexuality means therefore: to love oneself and the other.

Reflections and Discussion

■ Living and experiencing sexuality is not free from values:

• One can humiliate, devalue and degrade oneself and others
• Everybody is vulnerable in the sexual experience, sensitive touchable, susceptible
• One can cause pain in the sexual act to oneself and to the partner
• There are sexual plays which some may experience uncomfortable, annoying and intruding
• Sexual encounter can imply anxiety, shame, and feelings of inferiority
• Performance expectations about 'techniques' and intensity of orgasm cause pressure
• Human beings are never free from their sexual biography
• We all are more than a biological apparatus of lust, are a psychical-spiritual existence
• Foreplay is more than only increasing lust, it is a human confrontation

■ Human beings bring into the sexual play their psychical-spiritual wholeness and more than just a lustful acting; many elements are possible, for example:

• unconscious barricades and blockades	• unconscious parental control
• daily worries	• conditioned masks (to be attractive)
• ego-control and compulsion to hold back	• blocked self-expression
• romantic expectations	• expectations about life and partner
• saying 'yes' or 'no' to one's own	• rejection of feelings

body	
▪ inhibition of movements	▪ experiences about love and lack of love
▪ earlier experiences with men/women	▪ undeveloped sexuality (e.g. identity)

■ Sexual experience and acting imply also communication:

- How do you experience this?
- What do you like mostly?
- Do you like it now?
- How do you like to do it now?
- What touches you?
- Do you feel embarrassed with this?
- Show me how you like it!
- Take your time!
- I would like to try something new.
- What do you like mostly about me?
- Let's plan a weekend together!
- I feel sad; what is the matter with me?
- I would like to make a child now.
- Do you have an infectious illness?

■ Sexuality with personality education is more than creating lust and having orgasm. Saying 'yes' to sexuality is saying 'yes' to be a human existence with all the possibilities of sensual experiences.

The one, who really loves sexuality, creates it with self-reflection and communication with the partner.

Sexuality and eroticism regularly need a creative dealing, a thorough thinking and searching after oneself and the partner.

Diagram 1.28: Sexuality and Human Ecnounter

The sexual experience and acting in interplay with the human encounter in numerous versions:

Interest
Curiosity
Approach
Discovering the "you"
Dedication
Acceptance
Share
Participating

Encouragement
Eroticism
Falling in Love
Security
Confidence
Open for renewal
Experimenting

Nearness
Peace
Relaxation
Accepting lust
Excitement
Well being
Sensual experiences
Smooching

KEYNOTE:

We cannot and we must not always expect or demand, that sexual experiences and actions must take effect extensively in all components of sexual and human encounter.

It may be and it can be, depending on the situation, that one or the other component is at the center, while other components are in the background.

Sexuality and Love

- Sexual desire is in the opinion of most people bonded with love, so they assume erroneously, that they love each other when they want to possess each other.
- Sexual attraction produces for the moment the illusion of a unity, but without love after this 'unity' they remain aliens.
- Tenderness is the immediate expression of loving others.
- If it is really about love, erotic love implies a precondition: that my love expresses my (deepest) being - and that I experience the other in his being.
- To love a person isn't only a feeling - it is a decision, a judgment, a promise.
- The idea of a relationship which can be easily broken off if it isn't successful is similarly wrong like the idea that a relationship under no circumstances can be broken off.
- People, who meet each other lustfully, accept themselves as man and woman and strengthen their sexual identity.
- In the sexuality one encounters the other through the means of the body, and experience nearness and coziness.
- Happiness has to do with delightful and loving engagement for others.
- For people love is the centre of their life-project. Sexuality is a biological expression of love.
- The spiritual part of life can only be divided at the risk of destroying the unity and integrity of the whole human being.
- Many women reject consciously or unconsciously their sexual nature because they think, this would force them into a subservient attitude.
- No woman wants to have the feeling of being a sexual object.
- Searching lust is an expression of the vitality of orgasm.
- Excitement and movement are energetic phenomenon. Sexual drive is also an energetic phenomenon.
- Love and sexuality belong to the innermost core of each living organism. These give to life its meaning and produce the strongest motivation.
- The ability to reach satisfaction is a characteristic of a mature and realistic personality.
- Sex is of high interest for a child from birth and during long periods of his development.
- Babies can experience sensual lust through their body already from the first hour of their life. Not only through their sexual organs.
- The way to deal with sexuality during the childhood has a decisive influence on the later life of a child.
- The real life, the friendships of the adolescents, the relationship of the parents, their dealing with their children, the emotional atmosphere in the

family - all that has more lasting weight on the sexual behavior than what adolescents see on any screen.

- There is a form of love which slowly arises from eroticism and friendship. Thus, a love which doesn't appear as a unique immediate explosion between two unknown people, but where two human beings firstly meet on a sensible terrain of mutual estimation.
- The idealized presentation of love in the media doesn't prepare couples to deal with disappointments, frustrations and frictions.
- Specific individual attributes are decisive for a happy relationship: engagement, sensibility, generosity, consideration, loyalty, responsibility, trustworthiness.
- A decrease of sexual desire is caused by: changing of roles (to secure the income), stress at the work place, problems with health and misuse of stimulants.
- The most important factors are of a psychical nature: self-doubt, feeling of insufficiency, wrong ideals about one's own body, and fear of sexual performance, general interpersonal problems, and the different preferences about where, how, how long and how often.

➔ Self-love enables to love.

Marriage and Divorce

'Marriage' is a term with the core meaning: Going through the process of Individuation as man and woman (masculinity and femininity) to achieve the balanced union of the masculine and feminine archetypes (Anima and Animus), and in the mutual participation on this process. Sexual life is also a symbolic expression of this meaning.

'Marriage' in its core focuses from the psychical-spiritual view on these archetypal inner processes; and the meaning is 'archetypal-holy'; 'holy', because it is as an archetypal concept of the psyche unimpeachable. Only through this aspect 'marriage' as a ritual celebration and realization has its full legitimacy.

The 'homosexual marriage' has nothing in common with that meaning; the term 'marriage' is with no argument justified and as an archetypal meaning absolutely not legitimate (nonsense).

There are manifold causes forcing people to divorce, for instance:

- Unable to show one's own feelings and unable to solve problems
- Unable to argue and quarrel constructively

- The motivation to marry was out of fear of living alone and loneliness
- A conflict of mutual role expectations: e.g. caring and protecting
- Unable to listen and to talk (lack of ability to communicate)
- Lack of self-love and with that also an inability to love the partner
- The illusion that a marriage – a relationship – works from itself
- Unable to realize oneself genuinely (self-realization)
- Being victim and actor of the life lies and of the illusions of our Zeitgeist
- Professional and economical changes forcing the (moral) character
- Infidelity as a consequence of stagnating and superficial relationship
- A personal life crisis which the person can't or doesn't want to master
- A critical and impeded development of the character by one partner
- Inability to live sexuality and to deal with all its conflicts

Many people run away divorcing finally from one's self and self-responsibility. Probably 7 of 10 divorces have a solution; could be possible if both partners would learn with self-education and grow with individuation.

A first basic role is:

Each one is appealed to confront with himself without being manipulated or abused from the partner.

One's own dreams tell to each partner what he has to do and how he can grow with self-education and individuation.

A second basic role is:

Love demands the process of individuation from both.

Only if one partner refuses to fulfill the laws of love meanwhile the other follows that path fully self-responsible, divorce is appropriate.

A third basic role is:

If one partner doesn't want to go the path of individuation, the other partner has to start that process alone, and to demonstrate the positive value (as an alternative) compared with a path full of life lies.

One partner has to learn to love in order for the other partner to learn it too.

If these constructive basic roles don't help to succeed, divorce may be appropriate.

Divorce is also indicated if it becomes apparent that both partners had taken a wrong decision because they really don't go well together.

Sometimes divorce is a consequence of life circumstances, or because other persons destroy the love between both partners, or because both partners are broken down through a 'destiny strike', and then they don't have the force to recover and to renew their love.

Notes and Perspectives

What purpose does sexuality serve?

Write down the central keywords from this sub-chapter:

What is the human being without integrating positively sexuality and love?

Explain: Sexuality is important because…:

What did people learn about sexuality in their parent's home, at school and in the church?

What importance does sexuality have in the communication between life partners and in the interactions in general?

What kind of indirect relation exists between 'sexuality with love' and politics and the economy?

What does advertising impart to us about the unity of sexuality and love?

Formulate an important question about sexuality:

10.2. Sexual Experiencing and Acting

A marriage or a love-relationship is not simply a living-community with its own private interests.

Marriage or a love relationship is not a mere realization of love; and the meaning of marriage includes more than a human and juridical space to procreate and educate children.

A marriage or a love relationship is more than a common mastering of life. Marriage and love relationship are from its own genuine and psychological (- transcendental) meaning the process of self-growing through the opposite gender - cogent with the biological and psychological gender.

Based on this understanding of marriage and love relationship we can say: Coitus rarely requires a specific learning process. But that is not all of sexuality.

Sexual emancipation makes it possible to put the sexual act into a more manifold wholeness of sexual experience and creation. Nobody has to be embarrassed when we say that everybody can learn quite a lot about sexuality.

Tenderness can be rough or fine, in steps or shot forward, also displaced and cold. He who is tender, also wants to give a message with his caress.

Smooching can be like a child does with its mother and father. Smooching is, together with tenderness and experiencing nearness, also communication, just as directly with lovely and differentiated words. Why not think about what one wants to say to one's loved partner?

Physical nearness can convey important things about life: "I would like you to feel secure close to me", or "I accept you as you are". Intimate tenderness aims at more lust for experiencing and creating. Many forms are possible with empathizing and dosing, with joy of participating in the experience.

We can discover step by step how the skin, the senses and also the psyche react. Each experience of sensuality reaches the whole human being, is an experience of being here and being like that.

This demands concentration and devotion, understanding of the bodily and mimic reactions of the partner, the individual motifs also. Discovering and forming creatively and playfully gives joy. This can be learned.

There are many forms of sexual unification, objectively classified as 'techniques'.

Everybody can discover for himself many of those techniques with playful delight. Other things we may learn from books and magazines.

It may not be an aim to act acrobatically or vital to do extreme eccentric 'exercises'. However variation may be necessary.

To act on during years always the same pattern kills eroticism, causes boredom and flattens delight and joy. This way sex can't keep 'young'. Interest and curiosity are valuable drives to experience oneself and one's partner anew from time to time.

In the anonymity of the cities, the well-organized daily world and the offers for consumption a lack of creativity in the sexual experience and actions has a paralyzing effect with time.

We don't see this simply as a stimulant, but more as a conscious care for intimate encounter, as a consciously created variety of experiencing, the way we do it with eating, clothing and leisure activities. Of course problems will arise.

➔ To have a sympathetic understanding and learning about sexuality is essential.

Reflections and Discussion

■ We can widen our consciousness about sexual experience, and we can distinguish the experience itself:

- How does the skin react in different places to tender caress?
- How do I experience smooching and what do I like most?
- How do I like to experience and practice intimate contact?
- How do I kiss and what significance does kissing have during the love-play for me?
- Which kinds of touch do I like doing and experiencing especially?
- How can I let go and relax my mind during making love?
- Which given things by me and my partner have a disconcerting effect on my experience?
- What is rather repulsive, what do I not like to practice?

■ Eroticism isn't simply an appearance by accident, if specific feminine or masculine representations are given. Eroticism is an area of creating, in which the whole human being gives a self-expression, for example through:

- Acceptance of the own body (finding it good), of forms and sexuality
- Joy and genuine integration of lust-experience with all the manifold possibilities
- Positive thinking and feeling about oneself as psychical-spiritual wholeness
- Lust, curiosity and interest in 'seduction' - and this also after years of married life
- Ability to free oneself from daily matters, work, environment (others, rooms etc.)
- Self-confidence, positive self-esteem, delight in life in general

■ We can learn a lot about sexual practice:

- decorating the bedroom, the bathroom, the living room
- clothes for leisure which make you feel cozy and give sensual well-being
- music which generates relaxing associations and a well-doing atmosphere
- varied bed clothes (colors, textiles) and night-clothes (which give pleasure)
- expressions which are 'adult-like' and distinguished inform about feelings
- delight in initiative (e.g. also to go away with the partner for a weekend)
- spending love in manifold differentiated forms (love is more than a word)

■ Disturbances and difficulties in the sexual experiencing and acting are normal. They must have priority and should be discussed. Sometimes the subject is to identify in the biography, in the daily life or in psychical forces.

Diagram 1.29: The History of Sexual Experiences

The check list to look back on life:

Femininity of the mother/the sisters

Masculinity of the father/the brothers

One's own puberty

First love relationship

Separation, divorce

Lust and guilty feelings

Sexual difficulties

First sexual experiences

Most beautiful sexual experiences

Most painful sexual moments

Experiences with pornography

Failed love relationships

Dealing with masturbation

Religious sexual education

Education about femininity/masculinity

Sexual difficulties with the partner

First phase of menstruation/ejaculation

Self-experiences of virile power and inferiority

The one who elaborates his own sexual biography and reflects it yearly, can delight his sexuality in all life phases periodically. This is a path of being physically and psychically

The Biography of Sexual Development

To the sexual biography we can formulate questions for self-reflection:

1. Which partner (man, woman) influenced my life mainly?
2. What did I learn from my earlier partner(s)?
3. Which experiences are still in my memory as being embarrassing?
4. Which conflicts did I have in earlier relationships?
5. How did it come to separations?
6. How did my parents educate me to see men and women?
7. Which masculine and feminine aspects did my parents like especially?
8. How have I been enlightened on sexual matters?
9. How did I realize the sexuality of my parents?
10. How do my memories about my first sexual experiences still affect me?
11. Which attitudes about premarital sex did my parents have?
12. What did I like most about my earlier partner(s)?
13. What other sex-aspects do I see in myself looking back?
14. How did I react earlier to having children?
15. How did I experience jealousy (of my earlier partner)?
16. How did I experience my jealousy?
17. What hurt me especially about sexual experiences and activities?
18. How did I experience seminal fluid and ejaculation?
19. What does fidelity and 'being together in difficult times' mean for me?
20. What do I like especially about the masculine/feminine body?
21. How did I experience menstruation? (Man: What did I think about it?)
22. What didn't I dare to talk about with my partner?
23. What did my partners expect from me?
24. How did I speak with my partners about conflicts?
25. Which attitudes, dictates and prohibitions about sex did I experience?
26. Which feelings and experiences did I have about masturbation?
27. Which was one of the most beautiful sexual experiences in my life?
28. In case of abortion: How have I reconciled myself with that experience?
29. Which sexual prejudices did I have about men/women?
30. What was (is) the ideal about the body of women/men?
31. Which were the most embarrassing sexual experiences?
32. Which characteristics did I wish of my partners?
33. Which were the most beautiful non-sexual experiences with a partners?
34. How did I feel about my body during youth/young adult-time?
35. How do you feel about such questions?

The Functions of Sexuality

A human being is the sum of his life experiences, which are all assimilated into the personality and structure in the body. Life has a primary orientation:

It avoids the pain and strives for lust. This orientation has a biological nature because lust promotes, in physical view, life and well-being.

If a situation promises lust and threatens pain at the same time, and then we feel anxiety.

The formula of orgasm turns out to be the formula of life per se, in sexual reproduction, work, lust of life, mental (spiritual) productivity etc.

We consider the fact, that the sexual drive of human beings genuinely doesn't serve the aim for reproduction, but aims at specific kinds of increasing lust.

The sexual behavior of a human being is often exemplary for his other kind of reactions in the world. Of, the one who conquers (as man) rigidly his sexual object, we think him capable of the same careless energy also in pursuing other aims.

The one who renounces satisfying his strong sexual drives, in any considerations, will also behave in other parts of life rather concise and resigned than vigorous.

The education denies women the intellectual activity about sexual problems, for what they bring is the highest thirst for knowledge.

Unfortunately education of sex and eroticism is pursued only intellectually, disregarding completely the important feelings.

Such 'half-information', which exhausts in a bit anatomy and some gymnastic exercises and techniques, is in reality unfortunately often complemented by the fact that love and eroticism in our cramped civilization are not linked with joy and beauty but with anxiety, violence and criminality.

The suppressing of a harmonious and delightful sexual behavior destroys one of the biggest contra-weights against stress factors, which become even more difficult to deal with.

Sexuality is a life area where a person can express himself as a whole human being through for example:

- Accepting one's own body and forms of being and gender.
- Joy for lust and integration of living lust with all the manifold possibilities.
- Positive thoughts and feelings about oneself as a psychical-physical totality.
- Lust, curiosity and interest on seduction – and this also after years of relationship.
- Ability to become free of mental burden in daily life, work and environment.
- Self-confidence, positive self-esteem, lust on living in general (dedication for life).

Living and experiencing sexuality is not free of values:

- One can strengthen the partner and esteem him highly as a whole person.
- A person is in his sexual living more sensitive for being accepted.
- One can make through sexual behavior sincere joy for him and his partner.
- Sexual games can be really enjoyable, creative, cheerful and appropriate.
- Sexual encounter is an expression of trust, openness and dedication.
- To be free of a heavy (difficult) sexual biography is a great and vivid happiness.
- A person is a biological apparatus and also a psychical-spiritual being.
- The prelude is lust and increase of the whole human encounter.
- Living sexuality with the whole human being keeps oneself young.

➔ Sexuality is base and determination for a marriage and a love relationship.

Notes and Perspectives

What would change positively in daily life if human beings reflect profoundly on their sexual biography?

Write down the central keywords from this sub-chapter:

What is the human being without reflecting his sexual biography?

Explain: Reflecting about one's sexual biography is important because…:

What did people learn about sexual experiencing and acting in their parent's home, at school and in the church?

What importance does sexual biography have in the communication between life partners and in the interactions in general?

How do the people in politics and the economy demonstrate their sexual biography?

What does advertising impart to us about sexual experiencing and acting?

Formulate an important question about sexual biography:

10.3. Self-identity with Sexuality

'Self-identity' is a meaningful word. Basically it contains an image which everybody has about oneself. Identity means above all those formed aspects which remain constant during the years. To that belong: feelings towards one self, valuing one's own abilities, one's own peculiarities, the character etc.

Furthermore weakness, helplessness and ideas about one's own dealings in the world belong to that image. Self-identity is formed essentially at least as a specific character through the valuated own body sensation. Sexuality is a part of that.

We understand sexuality as a part of the self-identity in a wide range. Here is firstly the physical sensation in general: strength, stability, sensibility, corpulence and trouble proneness. Man and woman experience themselves with sexuality, with and without eroticism, with and without a sexually exciting and satisfying desire, with and without feelings of intimacy, of shame, of hygiene and of a concerned self-estimation.

Probably often comparison with the opposite sex takes place: penis-envy and inability to give birth are opposing, according to the psychoanalytical theory. The 'other' stimulates curiosity, interest, longing, lust or antipathy, depending on education and inner-psychical conflicts. Thus self-identity receives a contrasting tension: the complementary has to be found outside, has to be put in a relationship and to be lived as a partnership.

He, who can live that constructively, forms a healthy and stable self-identity.

Masculine and feminine sexuality are not the same. Sexual excitement occurs differently. Both partners can encounter each other actively, but the sensations about being together sexually are different. Penetration and incorporation stand in front of each other. Women want to be desired; men want to be allowed to desire. This forms psychical experience, the attractiveness and also the mutual fear of devotion.

In earlier times sexuality was restrictively understood as 'making babies'. All other was 'bad' or 'sinful'.

The reality today is: one to three times in a life a man and a woman beget a child. They may have during their life, sexual intercourse about 4000 times in total, preconditioned a 'good' relationship. That widens decisively the possibilities to build in sexuality into the self-identity.

Sexual identity is also a relation-identity; and: through the 'you' a human being becomes an 'I'. So man becomes sexually a man through a woman - and a woman finds here sexual self-identity fully through an intimate love-relationship. Through that both find acceptance and security in their masculinity and womanliness.

If the sexual self-identity is stable, then the sexual sensation and actions proceed securely, and then tenderness and love with sexual lust grow to a fulfilled happiness.

Reflections and Discussion

■ To self-identity belong many elements, along with the image about one's own general psychical force-system for example:

▪ experiencing health/suffering	▪ able for contact and relationship
▪ being happy/unhappy	▪ feeling of self-esteem
▪ level of self-control	▪ ideal about oneself
▪ ability to make decisions	▪ ability to undertake obligations
▪ devotion and self-assertion	▪ experience about actions
▪ autonomy and emancipation	▪ controlling / dominating environment
▪ ability for roles	▪ reflecting self-determination
▪ ability to deal with problems	▪ identification with one's own body

■ Aspects around sexuality which contribute to self-identity

▪ sensitivity	▪ excitability	▪ acceptance of desire
▪ experiencing orgasm	▪ ability to relax	▪ experiencing satisfaction
▪ fidelity	▪ ability to enjoy	▪ spontaneity
▪ honesty	▪ ability to self-expression	▪ overcome inhibitions
▪ ability to empathize	▪ vitality	▪ uncertainty

■ We can understand many sexual disturbances entirely as 'normal' problems in the forming of identity and finding of relationships.

It is wrong to expect, that self-identity has to be mature with the young adult-years. One shouldn't interpret each disturbance just as 'illness' and with that as 'therapy-need'.

To each psychical and psycho-physical and social process belong periods of crisis, of difficulties and suffering. In the long term happy sexual relations always go through processes of suffering.

■ Sexual disturbances like impotency, difficulties with orgasm and premature ejaculation are rarely organic problems. In general the causes are situated in the following areas:

▪ disturbance in relationship	▪ bonds to parents	▪ feeling of inferiority
▪ impatience, haste	▪ stress (work, leisure)	▪ wrong expectations
▪ contents of super-ego	▪ not integrated own nature	▪ fear of devotion/separation
▪ fear of life	▪ religious education	▪ lack of behavior-knowledge

Diagram 1.30: Questions about the Sexual Self-Identity

Self-reflection about forming self-identity on sexuality, on lust and love as a woman/man.

How do I experience my being a man/woman

How do I experience myself during intercourse?

What do I think about fidelity?

Do I have fear of separation/divorce?

Do I avoid human bonds?

How relaxed do I experience myself after sex?

How can I accept my drive-nature?

What importance does sexual pleasure have for me?

How do I experience the body odour of my partner?

What kind of hindrance do I have during sexual actions?

How is my dynamism in active-passive sexual practise?

How is my confidence in my sexual partner?

How can I deal with my mind-control?

Which sexual norms/ideals determine my actions?

What importance does being tender, smooching and petting have?

How can I speak with my partner about sexuality?

How spontaneous and creative am I during sexual plays?

What comes into my mind about my sexual biography?

How can I deal with symbiotical feelings?

Orgasm – Experiences and Drive-Theory

A lot of theories about orgasm and sexual drive exist. It seems here and there as if psychoanalysts, psychologists and sexologists haven't got over their own Christian education. They write similarly like priests after traditional sexual morality, only in a psychological vocabulary.

How can men speak about feminine orgasm, and what do feminists know about experiencing the orgasm of a man? Below, we present some theses, collected from different scientific literature, to inspire men and women to some reflections and to motivate them to talk about this further with the partner.

How is orgasm experienced? Sexology disagrees about this. But the diversity seems to be scientifically sure: once partially satisfied; once deeply fulfilled; once as an energetic explosion and thus as a relaxation; once as a feeling of un-fulfillment; there are obviously different 'grades of intensity'; a feeling of streaming, of clearness, of joy, of freedom, of heath, of distribution of the relaxing tension on the whole body; a lustful twitching in the whole body or a release in the pelvic.

Orgasm is on the one hand a biological sensation. On the other hand feelings essentially move the experience; a sensation of unity with the partner, with nature and even with the universe. Orgasm renews and revitalizes the physical sensation, evokes more deeply a feeling of 'belonging here' to the partner.

Feelings of happiness accompany orgasm, so they say. But, human beings don't seem to be happier, in spite of more open and free sexuality. Does the burden of the daily life have a stronger effect than this feeling of joy? Or doesn't this joy go really deep? Certainly, the physiological reactions, no matter how holistic physically, it says nothing about the psychical experience.

Men may have a reduced ability to feel and women may not be in the state to communicate with adequate words about their feelings, there may be a frame of the 'red-light-milieu' or a romantic room, yet always the whole human being is involved in the experience of the orgasm. We have on the one hand the vivid security, the speechless alienation or simply a sensual pleasure; on the other hand the human being with his biography is always a part of it. We lastly can't separate sexual lust from the biography and the psychical life.

It's obvious: If the biography isn't cleared out and the psychical life formed holistically and consciously, the sexual experience remains tied to the chains of the own history of life and to the chaotic psychical forces. This may obviously be the reason that there isn't more peace and happiness in society, in spite of sexual emancipation.

We accept the thesis, that the sexual drive itself produces an energetic tension, excitable through thoughts and fantasies, with external stimulus and contacts. The culminating sexual energy (called 'libido') pushes to increase the lust-sensation and 'explosion'. Both are experienced as lustful and want to be reached. This energy (or generally the sexual desire) is not 'dangerous'; it only becomes dangerous when human beings suppress this desire. The energy shifts, explodes in another way (e.g. violence) or causes psycho-somatic disturbances.

Sexual relaxation, being alone or with a partner, can create a well-being, doesn't have to be 'neurotic', and doesn't have to be devalued in any way. This model of drive is by no means 'vulgar', like traditional religious devaluations. It is also considerably 'derailed', if anyone declares, the urge for sexual relaxation is nothing else than a 'pressure-explosion' or 'the lust to do something forbidden'.

The body itself allows the human being to produce and to experience lust, and in that way to participate blissfully and with pleasure on the nature. We can practice sexuality completely differently, blind and unconscious, with feelings of guilt or embarrassment, or by saying 'yes' to one's own nature, with spirit, intelligence and heart.

Human Being with Sexuality

In a 'healthy' lived sexuality with a partner the human being experiences himself in his whole existence; in the same way he experiences his partner. Sexual lust grants social experience, self-reinforcement, and acceptance of the 'you'. Men may fix sexual lust more genitally. Women experience sexuality more holistic and more orientated on the relationship. But if man is educated as a personality, then it isn't true any more.

Both can thoroughly loose control for a moment during orgasm and both can thoroughly devote themselves to the sensation and the physical movements, by that 'forgetting all'. In the sexual being-together tenderness, security and nearness play a decisive role for the quality of the 'pure' sexual ('orgasmic') sensation. This experience can only be harmonious, if each can accept his body and at the same time the partner with their body. Each is attractive, lovable and worth living for the other.

These are not only classifications of psychical experience. A human with his entire existence is involved.

In this experience of existence the whole destiny of a human being is activated and given as a challenge. The whole psycho-sexual development from the earliest childhood is caught up with the sexual play, until this (history) in the unconscious (in the memory) can be put aside completely through individuation.

The human being experiences from birth in short life-phases increasingly nearness and distance, tenderness and harshness, contacts and movements of the body (e.g. rocking), embraces and rejections, lust sensations and privations, genital interests and reactions from the environment.

With all that a self-image is forming elementary, through the relation to father and mother also the wished image about an ideal partner, but also images about unacceptable partners.

"Do you love me?" is the first question from a child to her mother and father, already a prenatal experience. This question doesn't only concern love, but also equally the question about the 'me', that means: 'especially me'; 'me exclusively as your child'. Many parents have to deny this question more or less distinctively. In a relationship this question is repeated decisively; and with that often the drama of childhood.

The sexual play further more contains a series of behavior, from the foreplay to the fast increasing phase of excitement, to the orgasm and the time after. Each kind of contact and movement contains a message, for example:

"I like you (love you) very much." And: "I like your body odor."
"I want this caress to do you good."
"I feel deep confidence in you, and I feel how well I am opening myself to you."
"Relax now, release your thoughts and day-images, just feel now!"
"I feel your vitality agreeably, your physical strength, your energy."

"I can say 'yes' completely to you." And: "You and only you interest me."
"I want you to participate in my life."
"I enjoy with a deep acceptance your masculinity/your femininity."
"Let yourself be excited; it is joyful to experience you with your movements of lust."
"I discover you periodically new, your feelings, your sensibility..."
"I feel cozy and secure being with you."

People, who can share their sexuality with love and lust, experience genuine inner happiness. This certainly is always fragile and must be nourished, cared for, vitalized and protected.

He, who wants this happiness, is confronted with the question: "What do I want to invest, so that I can experience this happiness and this kind of human being?" A human being means by that: to grow with one's identity, to be open to change in all life-phases, but also to discover and to form oneself through the partner, to educate oneself in this process in the psycho-spiritual life.

This is a way of living existence, not just a 'sexual act'. The wish and the decision for that are the beginning, to elaborate the way to that happiness, alone and with the partner.

Notes and Perspectives

What purpose does a consciously formed sexual identity serve?

Write down the central keywords from this sub-chapter:

What is a human being without a sexual self-identity?

Explain: People's sexual identity is important because...:

What did people learn about being a human existence in living sexuality in their parent's home, at school and in the church?

What importance does the forming of sexual identity have in the communication between life partners and in the interactions in general?

What function does the sexual self-identity have in politics and the economy?

What does advertising impart to us about sexual self-identity?

Formulate an important question about sexual self-identity:

10.4. Exercises

1. What are your attitudes towards your sexuality, lived until today?

2. Which aspects of sexuality and forming your identity would you care for at the moment (learn)?

3. What kind of sexual memories can you not deal with well?

4. Communication about sex.

Mark an 'X' how the majority of people are treating (talking with) your their partner/friend, when they are in a fight (conflict) about a sexual matter and when you want to resolve it:

You can choose another theme of fight: ....

☐ convince	☐ sweep off his feet
☐ motivate	☐ manipulate
☐ encourage	☐ dominate
☐ valuate	☐ rival
☐ listening	☐ talk over
☐ questioning	☐ insulting
☐ directing	☐ vaguely intimate
☐ producing comfort	☐ inclined to be aggressive
☐ create orientation	☐ provoking
☐ investigate	☐ conquer
☐ understand	☐ evade, avoid
☐ giving support for decision	☐ covering
☐ make understood	☐ criticizing
☐ demonstrate interest	☐ nagging
☐ activate chances	☐ laud and angry
☐ in waiting position	☐ entertain
☐ reinforce	☐ harmonizing
☐ cooperate	☐ making enthusiastic

5. How to solve a sexual problem (or any kind of problems).

Write down a problem people (a person) may have:

....

What are the solutions until now?
Why does the person want to solve that problem?
Is the aim of the solution clearly determined?
What occurs, when the problem will never be solved?
Would other frame conditions chance the problem?
Are compromises possible?
Is the value of the problem rightly valued (importance, urgency)?
What does the person do to direct the problem towards a solution?
Are there other problems which are more important and have priority?

6. The development oft the sexual biography. Elaborate the following list of questions:

6.1. Which are for people in general the especially 'sensible' questions?
6.2. Why are these questions especially sensible?
6.3. Which aspects put most people in serious trouble?
6.4. What would people urgently like to clear out and resolve?
6.5. How do you think can people promote a process of change?
6.6. What can people talk about with their life partner/friend?
6.7. What can't people talk about with their life partner/friend?
6.8. Describe people's strengths in the whole field of attitudes, feelings, self-security, self-confidence, capacities, patterns of behavior, communication, openness, etc.
6.9. How does people's life partner/friend (today/in earlier times) accept (integrate) and respond to the strength of their partner?

Multiple Choice Test

Choose the four correct answers and mark them with a cross: ☒ a) lust

10.1. Aspects of value in sexual acting are:

☐ a) Time
☐ b) Room/place
☐ c) Confidence
☐ d) Openness
☐ e) Human encounter
☐ f) Sensation in general

10.2. The subject 'sexual experience and actions' allows the following statements:

☐ a) Everybody has his individual kinds of sexual sensation.
☐ b) In the sexual practice the whole biography of both partners comes into play.
☐ c) In the sexual act everything is always allowed.
☐ d) Eroticism is something that comes automatically and always by accident.
☐ e) Everybody can learn a lot about sexual practice, even after years.
☐ f) Not each 'disturbance' in the sexual experience and action can be named as 'ill'.

10.3. To the sexual self-identity for man and woman contributes:

☐ a) Without restraint
☐ b) Ingenious techniques
☐ c) Experience of satisfaction
☐ d) Experiencing orgasm
☐ e) Spontaneity
☐ f) Ability for creative expression